M000118633

BEYOND
THE
RATIONAL REALM

NANCY
God Bless!

NANCY
So, Love,

BEYOND
THE
RATIONAL REALM

LIFTING THE VEIL OF THE SPIRIT WORLD

JERRY MCDANIEL, CLAIRVOYANT

Wisdom House Books

BEYOND THE RATIONAL REALM

Copyright © 2020 by Jerry McDaniel
All rights reserved.

No part of this publication may be reproduced, stored in a retrieval system
or transmitted in any way by any means, electronic, mechanical, photocopy,
recording or otherwise without the prior permission of the author except
as provided by USA copyright law.

The opinions expressed by the author are not necessarily those of
Wisdom House Books, Inc.

Published by Wisdom House Books, Inc.
Chapel Hill, North Carolina 27516 USA
1.919.883.4669 | www.wisdomhousebooks.com

Wisdom House Books is committed to excellence in the publishing industry.

Book design copyright © 2020 by Wisdom House Books, Inc. All rights reserved.

Cover and Interior Design by Ted Ruybal

Published in the United States of America

Paperback ISBN: 978-0-9988261-2-7
LCCN: 2020913229

1. OCC003000 | BODY, MIND & SPIRIT / Channeling & Mediumship

2. OCC007000 | BODY, MIND & SPIRIT / Parapsychology / ESP
(Clairvoyance, Precognition, Telepathy)

First Edition

25 24 23 22 21 20 / 10 9 8 7 6 5 4 3 2 1

TABLE OF CONTENT

INTRODUCTION

To begin with, I would like to break down the title of this book.

BEYOND
"at or to the further side of"

RATIONAL
"based on or in accordance with reason or logic"

REALM
"a field or domain of activity or interest"

To put it in perspective, let us say the title heavily suggests that this book is about *going to the further side of logic to a field of activity or interest.*

The *interest* part depends on you and whether this subject matter is for you at this stage of your life.

This book might challenge you and push you in a new direction that will test the left side of your brain where logic resides.

The right side of your brain where forward thinking and imagination thrives might rejoice in this book, whereas the left side of your brain might get a little depressed knowing that logic will be tested and challenged.

Let me explain.

I'm a conservative Catholic who possesses an analytical, structured, scientific, and skeptical mind who wandered into the world of metaphysics by discovering gifts of mediumship, clairvoyance, psychic, and intuitive abilities in my mid-fifties, strictly by what I thought was accidental.

I did not grow up knowing I had these gifts unlike many other mediums, psychics, and clairvoyants who knew at an early age that they possessed special gifts. I did not grow up walking up to strangers telling them that "grandma says hello," as I disappeared into a fog or mist.

WHAT'S GOING ON?

See if any of the below applies to you . . .

You are standing in the kitchen and suddenly you see something out of the corner of your eye; you turn and look but there is nothing there.

You hear voices sometimes so clear that you swear someone else is in the house even though you are alone. You smell perfume that your mother use to wear, even though she died years ago.

You see the same sequence of numbers repeatedly on your watch, clock, and even the license plate on the car in front of you.

You have dreams of people, places, and things that you're not familiar with, only to experience some of those 'dreams' in the physical world.

You are not going crazy nor are your eyes deceiving you or playing tricks on you. You are not imagining things that you think are just not there.

THE UNEXPLAINABLE

What if there were worlds that we couldn't see, couldn't feel, and couldn't hear until we actually sat down for a moment and considered the possibilities that the reality that we know, which seems to be physical and rational, starts to give way to other 'realities' that seem to be non-physical and irrational?

Irrational, at least for the moment.

I've 'discovered' things that I cannot explain; experiences that I had never felt, gifts that I never knew I had, spiritual beings that are helping me that I never knew existed, and healing that I never knew could be possible. Consider the implications that some of the things you knew or thought you knew could be changed.

This thin veil between the physical world that we find ourselves in and the Spirit world can be lifted and explored if we're open to what lies beyond and if we're strong enough to accept it or at least keep an open mind about it.

To lift the veil, this book will explore a few 'strands' that are represented by areas of our everyday lives.

Reading how the Spirit world influences and impacts these areas you will start to part some of the strands that make up the veil.

The five 'strands' that this book will explore are . . .

- **RELIGION, VIBRATIONS, IMAGINATION, ENERGY, THOUGHTS.** There are a multitude of strands to investigate but these five are a good start as this is exactly where I started my journey.

There is also an opportunity to meditate on the ideas, information, and thoughts that will present themselves at the end of each of the chapters.

One last cautionary note . . . lifting the veil is not like flipping a light switch off and on. Think of it more like a dimmer switch; the more you turn the dimmer, the more it illuminates the area and awakens your sixth sense, but not all at once.

Having an awakening experience sometimes goes very slowly; so, go at your own pace, process what you see, hear, and experience, and enjoy your journey. Peace.

FOREWORDS

Jerry developed his spiritual abilities as a mature adult and therefore has the unique perspective of learning these skills step-by-step. An advantage of studying later in life is being acutely aware of the process. His unique path has translated into gifts for all of us; the ability to explain spiritual and other-worldly processes in an easy-to-understand, straightforward manner that takes the mystery and taboo out of the hidden, ancient world of the psychic medium.

Jerry adds another element to his work—the ability to connect with love on a soul level. His sincerity and devotion to all that is good reverberates throughout his endeavors, so that others feel safe and grounded during his heavenly work.

This book is truly a gift from Jerry's heart to yours, to be read, treasured, and read again. Let your head open to its knowledge and your heart open to its wisdom.

—Diane L. Ross M.A. / Hypnotist / Master Practitioner of NLP.

Author

Meditations for Miracles and Five Steps to Freedom

I knew from my first interaction with Jerry that he was blessed with a special gift.

His involvement in the Catholic church helps him relate to those unfamiliar with the process of mediumship, helping people feel comfortable in a realm that may seem eerie or disconcerting. He demystifies the mysterious.

Jerry's overall message is that we are eternal. **We continue even after we leave this earth. Love never dies. This book expresses these tenets through each relevant chapter offering practical ways to integrate the information for those at any level on their spiritual journey.**

—Mary Ellen Popyk

Executive Director of The Sanctuary for Mind, Body, Spirit
Publisher of Sanctuary Conscious Living Magazine

Chapter 1

IMAGINATION

"Imagination will often carry us to worlds that never were.
But without it we go nowhere."

—Carl Sagan—

Did That Just Happen?

I'm sure you've been on both ends of what I'm about to describe and that's when someone asks you to open a jar because the lid appears to be cemented on by a team of construction workers and it appears it's going to take a NASCAR pit crew to remove the lid.

You try to open it at first because you want to show everyone how strong you are and yet try as you may repeatedly, the lid is still sealed tight and not about to budge. You then proclaim to everyone that no one can get this lid off and that you're going to have to resort to desperate measures such as hitting it on its side with a hammer or beating it against the kitchen counter or better yet, drive around the neighborhood with the jar in tow.

Along comes a friend who says, "Let me try," and sure enough, two twists and it comes off easily, and much to your dismay he or she then prances around triumphantly as if they were on a parade float waving to their thousands of adoring fans.

Meanwhile, you sulk and slink and slither (sounds like a law firm) into another room, defeated and demoralized as you sink into a pit of despair wondering where in the world was your strength and your youth when you needed it?

To make matters worse, the person who twisted the lid off the jar is probably the person you like the least . . . just saying.

We've all been there numerous times in our lives and every time it happens, we must remind ourselves that it was a team effort as it did take someone to loosen the jar lid in order to twist it off.

The world of Spirit mirrors this activity in so many ways when it comes to loosening the jar. Spirit just loosens the jar for us, and it is up to us to use our imagination to figure out things…and may take several attempts to discover what lies beyond. In fact, by reading this, you could fall into any number of categories, one being the "I am curious" category.

You are curious about what is beyond what you know, beyond what you have experienced so far in your life, and beyond what you have been conditioned to comprehend.

You have been told that your mind is limited and along with your intelligence and imagination so just go along with society's flow of what is acceptable, and all will be well. But you want more than that and here you are. And I am here with you to tell you that not all that you see is what you see, not all that you hear is what you hear, and not all that you experience is what you experience.

For most of your lifetime, or at least since you were old enough to talk, the Universe has been loosening the jar for you so that when it's time, you make a few efforts to twist the lid and suddenly it comes off.

I've seen some incredible things, heard some incredible things, and experienced some incredible things simply because I finally chose to make the effort to twist the lid off a jar that I thought was forbidden and never to be touched, let alone removed.

I have witnessed people who have gone into trances and spoke different languages and given me advice and counsel and direction that came true strictly for my benefit. I have heard people speak my name at night when there is no one there and talk to me about things that are important in this world.

I know people who have communicated to beings from other galaxies and seen pictures of them as they have come from other dimensions to meet some of my friends.

I'm Scottish and Irish, born on St. Patrick's Day, and one of the greatest gifts I have ever received in my life is when I was presented at Christmas with a detailed genealogy of my father's side, going back some thirty-two generations. In this report I received some astounding news that I am a direct descendant of John Wallace who was the brother of William Wallace, Braveheart himself.

I love the movie *Braveheart*, and even though it could be classified as a historical fiction piece, it has some great moments. One such moment is when William Wallace announces he is going to invade England. The lords tell him that is impossible. His response is, "Why? Why is that impossible? Because you say it's impossible?" Or something to that effect. Wallace then reminds them of why they need to go do the impossible and the unthinkable because they've been suppressed for so long by the English that it's time to change that behavior in order to change the future.

And the only way to change the future for the Scottish people is to go do what must be done to obtain freedom. Freedom is what we all want and crave and desire, and by opening the jar you will start to catch a glimpse of what freedom looks like, universe style.

There is a saying that goes, "What would you do if you knew you would not fail?" It is a great line, but I would offer another line. What would you do if you knew there was no way of knowing how it would turn out or how it would affect your life?

There's no guarantee of what your reaction will be and how your life will be changed when you loosen the jar, but you will never know unless you take that leap of faith and grip the lid.

There will be several other jars to open as well but it all starts with one. Could this one jar of uncertainty lead to other puzzles in the Universe for you to solve or contemplate?

Nothing is impossible if we remove the blinders and, as Spirit tells me from time to time, take a leap of faith. The veil will get thinner and thinner the more you progress into the other side. Looking back at my own life I can say there were people, places, and things that the Universe put in my path that unbeknownst to me, were loosening the jar lid all along.

Think about the following story (that is true) for a moment and see what you think.

How do I purchase a brand-new house, that is slightly uneven at the end of the house where my office is? So slightly uneven that I did not even notice it; that is until I purchased a desk from a good friend of my wife's Kathy and put it in my office.

Once I did that, the desk drawer on my right side started to come open by itself. I scotch taped it but sometimes even that did not stop it from sliding partially open.

How is it that a random woman that was cleaning our house just happened to be a medium, and that the desk drawer just happened to come open as she was dusting it, and that just happened to open a conversation between her and me on mediumship?

I asked myself, did all of that just happen as a coincidence in which one domino fell and the rest followed suit, or was it something more? Take a guess as to which one I think it was.

TAKE FIVE

Take a deep breath and let it out with zero
expectations with this meditation; think about the
day before or the day of this meditation and ask
yourself the following question?

"Did that just happen?"

Relax and be pleasantly surprised at what
you receive.

Peace.

CROSSING THE BORDER

In the metaphysical sense, so many of us ignore or dismiss things that we cannot explain simply because they crossed our borders of thinking and we told them to go back.

Influences, such as the media, TV, books, movies, our friends and family, and society in general has shaped our thoughts that form a border of thinking that not only keeps things out, but also keeps you in. This brings us to the topic of imagination.

Things that we see, hear, feel, or experience that crosses our border of conventional thinking often results in a "no big deal…it is just something that I imagined." Only problem with that is, the border gets stronger and stronger because of the many thoughts and mindsets around imagination.

Imagination allows us to throw away conventional wisdom and thinking to cross the border into another dimension.

"I'm seeing things that aren't really there; I'm hearing things again; I must be going crazy." "What I witnessed didn't happen."

"My eyes are playing tricks on me."

The dismissal of the things that the Universe puts on our path in an attempt to get our attention continues to climb as we get older and that's because our filters become stronger and our borders stay up longer mainly because we don't want our lives turned upside down.

We become comfortable in our daily routines and push back on anything that will upset the apple cart. I go to work, come home, play with the kids, eat dinner, watch TV, and go to bed. I am content.

But the Universe does not want us to be content. The Universe wants us to be bold, daring, explore new paths, and find more peace and happiness on those new paths as well as great discoveries along the way.

Spirit has plans for us and the only way for these plans to rise to the surface is to send up signals from time to time so we can explore the possibilities of what our mission and purpose in life currently is and is to be in the near future.

The Temptations had a beautiful song when they sang "Just My Imagination." The lyrics state, "It's just my imagination, running away with me."

There is nothing wrong with your imagination running away with you . . . in fact, it is a key factor to helping us cross the border. After all, how can we start to believe in things metaphysical if we do not use at least a little bit of our imagination?

Look at these examples below, that have caused many people to pause and use their imagination.

- When you think of a loved one who has passed and suddenly you smell that loved one's perfume or pipe.

- When you think of someone whom you have not heard from in a while and suddenly the phone rings and it is that person.

- When you see a shadow out of the corner of your eye and it just so happens to be on the anniversary of a loved one who has passed.

Spirit reaches out to you to tell you that there is more to life than what you have come to understand. That the physical world isn't the rest of the iceberg underneath the surface, but the opposite is true in that the physical world that we find ourselves in is just the tip of the iceberg and what lies underneath is the realm of the Spirit world that needs to be explored.

Whenever you think your imagination is running away with you, catch up to it because you have a world that needs your attention and a life that needs to be explored. Everyone will benefit when you embrace your imagination. One's imagination will lead to more "what if?" scenarios where you experience more of what psychologists, college professors, and business leaders call 'lateral thinking.'

Lateral thinking is mainly mentioned in problem solving by offering solutions in a creative approach. This creative approach may also not use analytical and structured thinking along the way.

There are more than two ways to solve today's crisis and imagination will lead all of us to opening those doors so mankind will benefit.

- **MEDITATION**—sitting in silence will allow you to hear the voice of Spirit.

- **POSITIVE THOUGHTS**—begin and end the day thinking positively about something good that happened that day . . . something good always happens.

- **WHAT IF?**—think of what was once unobtainable and unachievable

TAKE FIVE

Take a deep breath and inhale anything that you
feel you need to explain but cannot and then exhale,
letting out a big breath sending the unexplained to
the Universe to be turned into a discovery.

Ask this of the Universe:

"Start me on the path of enlightenment so that
I might better understand."

Then relax and trust in anything you receive.

THE TRUTH IS IN HERE

I was a big fan of *The X-Files* and I remember the catch phrase of the show being, "The truth is out there." This is true for a great number of things including searching for answers to questions, etc. consider for a moment that 'out there' in a metaphysical sense means, 'in here.'

In here meaning your mind, body, and spirit.

In here means your intuition, which is the voice of your soul.

In here means the essence of what and who you have been in the past and what and who you are in this lifetime.

In here means pushing through the boundaries of religion to explore what spirituality is and what it means to you and those around you.

In here means putting aside those physical and mental diplomas of intelligence and education for a while and using your imagination to explore what lies beyond the conventional wisdom that you have been used to for so long.

In here means coming to the realization that you were a spirit long before you were a body or long before your body became a vessel for your spirit.

Time to use that imagination that I mentioned earlier.

Imagine this for a moment . . . your mind is composed of many chambers and inside these chambers are doors and beyond these doors are hallways. Down these hallways are rooms and inside these rooms are paintings on the wall. On these paintings are images of streets that can take you down avenues of wisdom, enlightenment, knowledge, light, energy, etc.

This illustration is meant to show you how deep your mind, your soul, your consciousness, and your light and energy is.

Think of the doors as portals that have no physical characteristics but just an entrance into other ways of thinking. Think of the hallways as pathways or passages without walls and without needing anyone's permission to walk down. Think of the paintings as memories of past lives or even where you currently are in this lifetime.

And think of the walls in the rooms as different colored rays of light that are just there to gently guide you wherever you want to go.

I once heard that once you remove the impossible, therein lies the truth.

The Universe does have structure but not physical structure. Beyond the realm of physicality does lie more truths and more knowledge and more wisdom but you must be prepared to put conventional wisdom aside at least for a moment.

After all, conventional wisdom is just that, a generally accepted theory or belief, an opinion, judgment, or prediction about a matter that is accepted by all or at least most all.

Coming to the realization that you hold within you the knowledge and wisdom of the Universe is radical thinking to be sure. We have heard all our lives that we are made in the image and likeness of our Creator.

If that is true, and I firmly believe it to be true, then is it so farfetched to believe that we have, as the great Franciscan priest, author, and lecturer, Richard Rohr puts it, "The DNA of the divine within us?"

Once you just sit down and think about this for a moment, you will possibly start to explore those chambers in your mind. Once you do, be prepared to meet your soul, your essence, your consciousness, your Higher Self, which is the true essence of who you are as a sacred being, for you cannot explore these chambers without your Spirit.

Therefore, we refer to ourselves as mind, body, and Spirit. It is the image of a tripod and when one leg is weak, the foundation for a spirit-filled and meaningful and mindful life is not on solid footing. (Thank you Cursillo for that analogy.)

It is like when we dream. When we dream, there's no place we can't go; there's no one living or deceased that we cannot meet, and there's no situation that poses a threat to our well-being . . . at least if we wake up in time and if we have said a prayer of protection before we go to sleep.

To do all of this requires the one thing that Albert Einstein said was more important than intelligence: *imagination*. Use your imagination to push beyond and cross the border that you have carved out for yourself and that others have placed inside your head.

Inside, not outside. Go within and discover what once was undiscoverable.

TAKE FIVE

Take a deep, deep breath and let it out, exhaling,
and leaving the worries of the day behind you.

Ask this question:

"Spirit, can you help me cross the border and draw
me closer to you to experience the Universe?"

Close your eyes and be at peace.

HARD TO BELIEVE WHAT CANNOT BE CONCEIVED

The term is 'surreal', and it is used time and time again when people see, hear, or experience something that does not seem real. It has been used to describe certain situations that people find themselves in when they cannot believe what their five senses are telling or showing them.

The spirit world could very well fit into the surreal category because to lift the veil into this realm you will need to start to deemphasize your five senses and focus as much as you can on your sixth sense. This will take time, effort, and patience, but you will get there.

It will also take practice and silence and a willingness to believe and trust.

When it comes to conceiving things that perhaps we had not thought of conceiving before, visualization is one of the keys. Many times, in our lives either we have told others or had others tell us to visualize this or that. It could be a cruise, or a new home, or 'success'. It could be something crystal clear or it could be so foggy, so muddy, that visualizing seems impossible.

If you want to visualize something funny here is one for you. When I first tried to visualize anything remotely linked to the other side, I would close my eyes and squint real hard . . . as if that were going to work. I get it when you are squinting at the sun but where does squint-ing come into play as you are closing your eyes? I tried and tried and tried and for the longest time nothing worked. I saw little during any mediations or development circles that I was attending.

I am again going to turn to the Christian author, lecturer, and mystic Richard Rohr, who said, "Don't try harder, surrender more." I wish I had heard that years ago instead of just the other day during one of his recorded lectures.

Sometimes we want something so badly that we simply try too hard and try to chase it more than it chases us.

Often in our lives we have heard the phrase, "Seeing is believing." Even that one I have a hard time with since our eyes seem to play tricks on us. What is it then, that we have a hard time believing? UFOs, aliens, life on other planets, talking to people who have passed, psychic abilities, ESP . . . the list is endless simply because we have not had the right amount of exposure to these areas and more.

My task with this book, as Spirit has told me, is to reach out via my writings and get everyday people (of which I am one) to develop and hopefully keep an open mind on the material presented. How in the world do you converse with people who are no longer breathing? How can you think of something and someone else says it? How can you tell someone things that only they know?

What happens in most cases are pre-determined notions or ideas which have been already formed.

These ideas are preventing us from expanding our mind to learn more truths.

When we think of things and whether to accept or reject them, our thoughts fall into one of three arenas. These arenas are:

- **(MIS) UNDERSTANDING**

- **(NO) PERCEIVED VALUE**

- **(NO) PERCEIVED NEED**

Looking at each one, which by the way are the three arenas of negotiating or thinking as taught by the training director (Dr. Noswal) at the company that I used to work for, perhaps we can see the obstacles into accepting new ideas and a possible new way of thinking.

- **MISUNDERSTANDING**—You have been told some truths over the years from the world of Spirit in small fragments like pieces of a puzzle, but your mind is dismissing them because this is simply a case of misunderstanding on what you've been programmed to believe…or so your mind thinks it is. You have come to some sort of conclusion based upon tidbits here and there and you have quickly surmised that it just is not for you.

Perhaps little by little though some of these fragments of clarity have been seeping through and have brought you to this point.

You can thank your Higher Self for this introduction to awakening, and if you have already been awake then there is more for you to discover.

- **NO PERCEIVED VALUE**—Perhaps you have glanced at some of the ideas that have come across your vast mindful landscape regarding things that seemed impossible or highly unlikely. When our thoughts enter the arena of NO PERCEIVED VALUE, we are dealing with past experiences

In other words, someone once told us or tried to show us some information that dealt with the Spirit world or metaphysical gifts and we just didn't pay much attention to the information or we just dismissed it as heresy and nonsense. Could be that we were exposed to these subject matters on TV, etc. or a magazine that highlighted this information.

After these 'encounters,' you've concluded that it's not for you, especially if you've talked to someone who deems themselves to be a Biblical scholar or religious figure and they've indicated to you that it's from the dark side, even though nothing could be further from the truth. This journey into the realm of Spirit is one of the most spiritual and mystical journeys you will ever undertake.

- **NO PERCEIVED NEED**—Things have been going so well for you that you have decided you simply do not need this in your life at this point or any other point for that matter. You do not see a need for this intrusion into your daily routines, an intrusion that will shake up the path you are on, so why bother upsetting the applecart? There are numerous problems with that mindset. First, your daily routines are exactly that... routine. You are in a rut, but it is a comfortable rut, and you are not about to climb out of it because that calls for way too much effort at this point in your life that you are not willing to exert.

Second, the applecart is an illusion because of what society deems acceptable and unacceptable; so, you just go along with the flow of the crowd because it is the way you've always been and the way you were taught when you were young. Going against the flow of the crowd is too hard and too exhausting.

Third, there is a tremendous need for connecting to the other side; because the other side is full of wisdom and knowledge that is free from discrimination and free from worry.

Thinking of the impossible as possible and thinking of the unlikely as likely will start to put you on a path of conceiving and that's where our belief systems will be turned around and start to head in a new direction.

TAKE FIVE

Take a deep breath and exhale all the anxieties of the day . . . those anxieties do not own you nor have possession of your life. You do.

Ask yourself this question:

"Is there anything to fear or be afraid of beyond this physical earth?"

Relax, close your eyes, and sit there for a few minutes and listen.

And listen and listen.

Chapter 2

THOUGHTS

"We are addicted to our thoughts.
We cannot change anything if we cannot change our thinking."
—Santosh Kalwar—

AROUND HERE, THE DEAD DON'T DIE

There are several mindsets and opinions on what happens when we die. Some say that is it and there is nothing after this lifetime so enjoy it now while you can. Some indicate that you're in a sort of holding pattern until either Jesus comes again or until more awakening happens, then again others such as Spiritualists talk about the 'continuity of life' and how important it is to show that our loved ones can communicate with us.

Being brought up Christian, there was the teaching in Sunday school of life after death, depending upon what kind of life you have led on Earth. There is a myriad of opinions regarding what exactly transpires when our heart stops beating.

There is life after death; the continuity of life does continue although in different forms and we can communicate with those loved ones who have passed.

Some call it channeling, while others call it connecting, but whatever you call it, I'm here to tell you that life never dies, and the afterlife does exist.

The first time I channeled or connected to someone who had passed, I was beyond stunned. I did not see the person that clearly, I just knew he was there.

I kept thinking, "Is this really happening?" And yet, there he was.

But as soon as I 'saw' him, a problem quickly arose as my mind started to form an intervention on my gifts of mediumship.

The structured and analytical part of my brain started to push back hard telling me that I was just imagining things and wanted this to happen so badly that I had created this image of a 'dead' person.

I am not sure what all is on my bucket list, but I know for a fact that creating an image of a 'dead' person is not on there. Trust me.

Whenever we lose a loved one, we mourn, grieve, cry, get angry, etc.

We look back on the good times and the not so good times.

We ask ourselves, "Was there anything I could've done to have made their life better or to have eased their pain?"

We start to question everything we did and did not do.

Sometimes we point fingers at ourselves and accept blame for their passing, even if no one is pointing the finger at us, or whispering in low tones in the corner of the funeral home about how we should have done more.

We move on the best that we can. To be perfectly honest, it is difficult sometimes to tell someone who is sitting across from me, that it is going to be okay as I look at the circumstances of their loved ones passing. It is even harder to tell people to move on because let's face it, it is easier said than done.

This is exactly why communicating with those who are on the other side of the veil is important and so needed in today's world.

We want to know that they are okay and not in pain. We want to gain some sort of closure on their passing. We want to receive validation that they are proud of us.

We want to say the things that we did not get to say. We want to gain insight.

Some just want to know if their loved ones in the Spirit world still love them.

It is funny how some fundamentalists look at communicating with the 'dead' as a sin and something never to be practiced.

It is funny because communication comes in many different forms- not just verbal.

Consider this . . . when we think of a loved one or of something that they used to do, we are communicating with them via thoughts and frequency.

When we remember them either on their birthday or the anniversary of their passing, we are communicating with them via a memory or emotion.

When we touch a physical object and instantly think of them and smile, we are communicating with them via vibrations.

Or when we just do, see, or hear something and say, "Dad, you would have loved this." . . . yes, we are communicating with them via verbal.

In Hinduism, one of the core beliefs is that the individual soul is immortal. Most major religions whether of an Eastern or Western origin believe that there is life after death.

In Christianity and Western Protestant religions, the entire modus operandi hinges on being 'saved' so that when one dies, one does not go to Hell, but Heaven, and is reunited with others who were 'saved.'

When people see that I am a medium and that I talk to people who have passed, suddenly, I am treading on dangerous ground; sacred ground that most organized Western religions deem a sin.

They never stop and think about the countless times they've reached out to their loved ones to ask for advice when they're stuck, thank them for watching out for them, or just to say hi to mom and dad when they see something that stirs up a memory.

I know a ton of people (and probably so do you) who talk to their loved ones every day in passing or at least feel them nearby from time to time.

How is that any different than having gifts of mediumship?

We do not seem to spend time attempting to understand metaphysical gifts such as mediumship . . . we instead reach a conclusion based on fear. We separate ourselves from those things we fear, attach a label to those things we fear, and the person that happens to 'possess' those things we fear, we immediately dismiss them as somebody or someone to be shunned, ignored, and possibly isolated.

When that happens, it starts to represent a spiritual mob mentality.

This has happened in my own church.

I sit at the back because I know there are people several rows ahead of me that have talked about me and my gifts negatively and choose to not engage me in conversation, so I choose to sit there and worship God.

Just sitting there in the presence of the Divine One makes me feel alive and transformed and isn't that how we are supposed to feel, transformed somehow?

The transformation of me over the years since I peeked behind the veil has done nothing but draw me closer to the Divine. Has drawn me closer to God like never before.

Gifts are meant to be shared and not put in a box just so people can feel at ease. When used correctly in a spiritual way and for the highest good, mediumship is a treasured gift from God.

Communicating with those who have passed is a beautiful and inspiring thing.

I have a two-hour weekly radio show in Orlando in which I discuss things that are of a metaphysical nature and do live readings over the air.

It has been a tremendous blessing in my life and in the lives of many others who call in.

To set the stage, I have three screens in front of me; the screen on the left lists the people calling in, where they are from, and what they are calling about. The screen on the right features people who prefer to text me questions about loved ones or guidance they need on the path they are on instead of calling in.

The screen in the middle is where my microphone is, so I do not use that screen. With my ADD, two screens, paper and pen in front of me to take notes, a script that I sometimes use with bullet points as reminders on various segments coming up, the producer talking in my ear, and the big clock in front of me that keeps me on time, I have more than enough to keep me busy.

One evening as I was wrapping up the show, I saw that there was still one person I had not gotten to; a man holding on the line, wanting to talk to his deceased son. I could not go over my time because there was another talk show coming up in the studio where I broadcast from.

It was after 10 p.m. and I was not feeling well, just having gotten over pneumonia and bronchitis, but God was telling me to take the call off the air, which I sometimes do. I told the man, whom I will refer to as D, that I would take his call off the air in another studio.

I took his call and he wanted to connect with his deceased son so I said I will give it a try as I do not promise folks that the loved ones they want to connect to will come through. It just does not work that way. The loved ones who come through are the ones who are meant to come through.

I focused and told D that I did see a male coming through who looked young and was holding a skateboard. I indicated that he looked to be in his late teens or early twenties. D broke down crying saying that it was his son who died at twenty-two years old and used to be heavy into skateboarding.

You could feel the man's pain as he was literally sobbing as he told me his son had been murdered just a few months earlier. His son assured his dad that he was at peace, that he was a great dad, and to not worry about him that justice would eventually be served.

I could visualize D's shoulders just relaxing as I translated some incredibly beautiful messages from his son. All D wanted was to connect and tell his son that he loved him, and the Universe gave him that opportunity.

You will never convince me that incidents like that are not from the highest source . . . ever. These gifts and other mystical events that happen beyond the veil are of a deep and spiritual nature.

Sometimes that which we do not understand can draw us closer to the Universe if we just relax and allow it to happen in a non-judgmental way.

TAKE FIVE

Take a deep breath inhaling the pressures of the day and exhaling them back out into the Universe to allow positive energies to transform them into something beautiful.

Ask yourself this question:

"If I could talk to just one person that has crossed over, who would it be and what would I say?"

Close your eyes thinking of that person and take as long as you need manifesting your love for the one who has crossed over to the other side. Now say what you want to say and know that your loved one is near.

Peace.

IS ANYONE LISTENING?

With my gifts, I get a ton of questions. "Will I find love?" "Will I find peace and happiness?"

"What does my future hold?" "Is my health okay?" "Will I be successful?" "Will my finances be okay?"

These questions are perfectly normal and understandable.

I have questions as well.

The questions are fair, sometimes simple, but other times complex. The future is scary and uncertain and sometimes we are afraid to face what we do not know and what we do know.

But we are not meant to know everything and that is for any number of obvious reasons. Lifting the veil of the spirit world will not give you everything you need to live your life currently and in the future.

We are meant to live our lives embracing every day as an adventure, something to look forward to even if we do not know what's going to happen. Not follow a script, reciting lines that have been given to us, and playing out scenes that we believe we are to play.

Yes, I have questions.

What if on Christmas morning you woke up knowing exactly what Santa was going to bring you? You already knew all the presents that you were going to get, etc.

There is a certain joy and wonderment in not knowing everything about the future.

Sometimes we must quit asking questions and listen.

We cannot hear the answers if we spend all our time asking questions. And sometimes when we ask questions, we hear nothing but silence. And in silence we can still hear answers even though they may not be the answers we seek.

I have permission to tell the following story.

I gave a reading once to an impressive young lady; we will simply call her Diana. The reading was going well, and Spirit came through with multiple validations. I received information about her sisters, one who had a medical issue.

The other sister, whom we will call Shelli, was acknowledged as being somewhat of a clown and a cut up and a great sense of humor full of life and energy.

Both observations from Spirit were spot on.

Shortly after the reading, however, Shelli the one who was so full of life, suddenly came down sick . . . extremely sick.

So sick that she landed in the hospital and her health declined so rapidly and quickly that it took your breath away.

She even asked Diana, "Did Jerry get the reading wrong? Did he mean me when he talked about someone having medical issues?" She asked this, even though she knew it was her other sister who had multiple sclerosis that Spirit identified.

Tragically within a manner of days, she passed.

So, what are my questions?

Regarding Shelli, I have a ton of questions for Spirit.

First, why? With my gifts, why couldn't I have seen this or even had a clue as to what was going on medically with Shelli?

Second, tell me God, what is the use of having these gifts if I cannot save a person?

Third, why did Shelli seemingly in the prime of her life and with young children and a husband get taken from her family and friends with no warning?

Spirit revealed to me a few things, one of which was telling me it is hard to hear answers when I (Jerry) am so busy talking.

So, I became quiet. Here are the lessons I learned.

Yes, I have a special gift, but I am not the only one who has these gifts. A quick reminder that on numerous occasions I have told a multitude of folks that "we're not meant to know everything."

I am not meant to save people with my gifts; I am meant to help heal people and assist them on their path. It is up to me to use the gifts that I have been given to help people heal by the grace, enlightenment, and awareness from the Universe, from Spirit.

I am meant to see what I am meant to see, nothing more, nothing less.

I relayed info as I saw it . . . could it be that some of my messages had special meaning for more than just one person?

And finally, could it be that I'm not perfect all the time with my messages? Possessing these gifts will not make me perfect.

Know that Shelli is close to Spirit as much as Spirit is close to her.

She is safe and happy and at peace.

Lessons learned.

One more lesson that might help you on your path.

STOP—for a moment and just concentrate on breathing.

LOOK—for the moment when you hear, see, or feel the voice of the Universe.

LISTEN—to what Spirit has to say . . . to you and only you.

Someone is always listening. And listening and listening. I have said it a ton of times, "When we hear nothing is when we hear everything."

I am not talking about eavesdropping; I am talking about truly listening and knowing our desires, ambitions, wishes—everything.

Speaking of listening, it is my belief that the Universe does not eavesdrop in our conversations every now and then only to pick up a few snippets that it can piece together to conclude if something is wrong or not.

This is not *CSI: Universe.*

It is perfectly ok to put things out into the Universe via thoughts, words, actions, deeds, writings, etc. as a way of acknowledging what we do want to happen in our lives. Putting things out into the Universe is a beautiful way of making those things that we want, desire, and wish for even more impactful.

As the great inspirational speaker Esther Hicks once said, "Wish for those things that we want to happen, not the things that we DON'T want to happen." At the end of the day, positivity always trumps the negative thoughts and words in our lives.

TAKE FIVE

This will be a different one, but Spirit wants me to write this. Breathe in deeply the things we do not want to happen and let out a huge exhale, breathing out those things that we DO want to happen and send them out into the Universe.

Try saying this to the Universe:

"I would like this to happen in my life . . ." then think of one thing that you would like to have happen in your life, not putting any time restrictions on it.

Close your eyes and let the Universe take that one thing and 'work' on it.

IT'S NOT WHAT YOU THINK

We have heard a million times, "It's not what you think, it's what you do."

That could be true but follow me for just a moment. I had a thirty-five-year career in sales and for several years at our Lake Tahoe sales meetings, we had guest speakers.

From Dick Vitale to Rocky Bleier, to inspirational and motivational speakers and leaders, we ran the gauntlet of people who came to talk and inspire us.

One person has stood out to me, even though I cannot recall his name. This sales meeting was many memories ago but, like all our sales meetings, it was impactful. The person was a National Geographic explorer.

He brought with him slides (back in the day before PowerPoint) and showed us some amazing pictures of his travels in the snow-covered mountains that he and some of his companions climbed. He was a well-traveled and experienced expeditioner.

He told a tale of one of his best friends throughout his presentation only to reveal at the end that his friend had perished in a mountain climbing expedition. It was an amazing presentation, but not from that standpoint. It was some of his final words that I remembered the most.

His last quote was *"your beliefs drive your behavior"* which for me was such an epiphany that I immediately wrote it down. I have quoted it so much since then that it has become part of who I am when I do my metaphysical work.

However, I do want to add something to that quote.

*"Your beliefs drive your behavior and your thoughts
drive your beliefs."*
—National Geographic Explorer & Jerry McDaniel.—

Our thoughts tell us who and what we are and what we believe and do not believe. Yes, we can put our thoughts on a different path (it is called learning) and change our belief systems which will drive our behavior, hopefully towards a more positive path that will help people.

But most of the time, we are just fooling ourselves if we believe we can act opposite of what we think.

Sure, there are those times when we act other than what we think, but those are exceptions and not the rule.

Thoughts are energy and vibrations and the more positive thoughts we can 'put out' into the Universe, the better. It is a manner of keeping our thoughts pure, honest, and positive.

So, it IS what you think mainly because your thoughts and my thoughts are what drives us to behave the way we behave.

What does this have to do with the rational realm that we find ourselves in? The best way to describe it is this: in our world we deal with physical things that we can see and touch. We do not deal very well with things that are 'in the air' such as thoughts.

We cannot see and touch our thoughts (even though folks like me do have that ability) and so we tend to not think of them as energy and/ or vibrations.

But our thoughts are just as powerful as words that come out from our mouths or the actions that define the words.

When we think of our loved ones, they hear it just as they would hear the spoken word. Light, energy, vibrations are all attached to the thoughtful word in this case.

For years, I was involved in a ministry that implemented weekend retreats for men. These retreats involved talks, spiritual exercises, mass, etc. These retreats were to lead the men into a lifelong involvement in this movement. I still meet with a group of men on Saturday mornings because of these weekends even though it has been over thirty years since my first weekend.

One of the talks that is given is the very first talk of the weekend. It is called the IDEAL talk and it basically says where your money goes, where your time goes, and where your THOUGHTS go . . . there goes your ideal.

Basically, saying what we spend our time doing, what we spend our money on, and what we think about goes a long way to defining the kind of person we are and what we think about life.

This begs the question: where do your thoughts go? Is it full of negativity or is it focused on more positive thinking? Where your thoughts go, there goes your ideal. Might be time for a paradigm shift depending upon what and how you think. What do you think about? What consumes your thoughts during the day? If you were to keep a scorecard during the day of your thoughts, positive on the left and negative on the right, what would that scorecard look like?

A long time ago I worked for a merchandising company that created displays for the liquor industry. We would set up displays in stores and every year we would go to conventions and set up huge mock rooms so the sales teams could see their various brands merchandised.

I met some neat people and one of those people was a man named Richard who came from the Boston area. We became great friends so much so, that his family came and stayed with us in Florida during one of their vacations.

During a break at a convention in Las Vegas, he wanted to show me the power of positive thinking and the reverse power of negative thoughts.

He had me hold out my arms straight and asked me to think of a negative thought. I could not think of anything negative (I was so young and naïve back then) so he said, "That's great Jerry." He gently put his hands on my arms, and I could not move my arms down.

Then he said, "What if something happened to Mary and Katie, your daughter?" Instantly, he barely touched my arms and they fell, demonstrating the power of negative thoughts and how it can affect everything we do. That demonstration has stayed in mind for decades now and is a point that needs to be made repeatedly. Think positive thoughts and yes, happy thoughts.

TAKE FIVE

We all have SPIRIT GUIDES who help us on our path(s) in this lifetime.

You have them and so do I and in time they will reveal themselves to you if they have not done so already. Normally, there is one main guide who helps you.

This will change over time and depending upon where you are in life another main guide may step in to help you with that part of your spiritual journey.

Here we go:

Take a deep breath, breathing in the negative thoughts of the day and send them out into the Universe so they can be turned into positive thoughts.

Put this comment to your Spirit Guide:

"Help me turn my negative thoughts into more positive energy."

Then close your eyes and think nothing but good . . . enjoy.

NAVIGATING THE NARROW-MINDED PATH

I used to work for an amazing privately-owned company that had such an impact on my life that I still fondly remember the co-workers, the sales meetings, the workshops, the training, and the impact that our small little company had on the industry.

We were an aggressive sales-oriented company that worked hard but had so much fun it did not seem like work half of the time. One of the great things about this company was that the owner, who was a tremendous individual and true entrepreneur, had a great mantra for our company.

It was the poem by Robert Frost, "The Road Not Taken". It was our 'battle' cry because we did things in the marketplace that seemed so unconventional. We traveled and never swayed from that road.

The fruits of our labor were on this road that nobody else wanted to embark on because it was a tough, hard road. We made many discoveries and created many wonderful products and programs and enabled so many people to enjoy fruitful lives on this road, or path that at the end of the day it was all worth it.

THE ROAD NOT TAKEN is the path that has created most of the leaders in our world simply because they saw things that no one else did. On this road or path are visions for those that recognize it and embrace it.

Great discoveries are never made on paths that are well-traveled but believe it or not the paths that are well-traveled are the ones that are the widest.

That is because those people who travel on that path find it nice, comfortable, big, non-threatening . . . soft, warm, and most of all inviting. Let us face it, it is the path that is the most attractive.

The narrow paths are the ones that are unattractive, ugly, full of weeds, undeveloped, overgrown, full of dirt, and rocks, and potholes.

Those paths are just waiting for people to take the leap of faith and explore. They are narrow for a reason and it is not because of the mindset of the people that dare to walk down the path. It is because so few people have wandered onto this path.

These are the paths to discovery; awareness, enlightenment, knowledge, imagination, and wisdom, and the only way for these paths to widen so more people can walk on them, is for you to take the first step.

This path is one that few people covet, which explains its condition.

It is kind of ironic that people who travel on the big, well-traveled paths are those who sometimes have the narrowest of mindsets. And the people that take a bold step often take on the narrowest of paths because they know that wondrous discoveries lie just around the bend.

Narrow-mindedness is destroying cultures, spirituality, development, mindsets, progress . . . etc. Narrow-mindedness is a disease that plagues this world.

Narrow-mindedness puts labels on people, places, things, ideologies, etc. and then puts those labels in a box on a shelf hopefully to be forgotten.

Part of my calling with my gifts is to help people on their paths.

Most of the time with the readings I give, I see two paths that represent the past and the present. Spirit then shows me at least one new path for the future and it is my calling to show people the path(s) that the Universe is giving them a sneak peek at.

How would we ever know what failure truly looks like if we do not try at those things that have such a low percentage of success that most would never dare try them?

It is a radical approach to finding one's purpose and mission in life, I will give you that.

Back to that little company I worked for. We tried so many things in the marketplace that just did not work it was almost comical.

But the flip side of the coin was, we came closer and closer to the business model that we all knew would succeed if we could just get close enough to develop it and implement it.

And we did.

It became a huge success because of our vision of what success should look like.

There is even a book that has been written about this company called *Billion Dollar Kibble* by Christie Cooper and Mary Hooks.

Everything starts with an idea; a vision, a purpose, and a mission. Spirit encourages those sitting in front of me to start a new career or to start a company.

We can create vision and possible enlightenment on an overgrown, rock-filled, narrow path.

Deep within you there is a path that you have been dying to take but you're hesitant because the other path looks so inviting.

Hopefully, it is time to choose the path that the Universe wants you to check out.

No one put it better than Robert Frost.

"I shall be telling this with a sigh
Somewhere ages and ages hence:
Two roads diverged in a wood, and I—
I took the one less traveled by,
And that has made all the difference."

TAKE FIVE

Take a deep breath and breathe in the anxieties of taking on a new path and breathe out that anxiety for the Universe to ease your fears and concerns.

Ask God this question for contemplation:

"Is there a path that needs my attention?"

Close your eyes as this could be the first of many requests of the Universe.

METANOIA

For the skeptics in the world, of which I used to be one, pause while we ponder some thoughts.

Did we really land on the moon? There's compelling evidence amongst conspiracy theorists that suggests we never landed on the moon. A government cover up that served only to show the Russians we could beat them in the space race and make a strong case for increased budgets for NASA.

Was there more than one shooter who assassinated President Kennedy? Again. More compelling evidence such as the grassy knoll, the eyewitnesses who swear shots came from two different areas, the Russian connection (why does everything seem to suggest Russia?), and the single-bullet theory.

Was 9/11 a government cover-up to increase budgets to fight terrorism? Again, skeptics point to video evidence to suggest that the planes did not hit the twin towers, etc.

And . . . can a person really receive messages from people who have died?

Think about it for a moment. People whose hearts have stopped beating and have gone on before us can still communicate with us. That is some crazy #@*%!

After all, mediums are nothing but con artists who prey upon honest, good, hard-working folks who have lost loved ones and are just ripe for the picking, right?

Absolutely not. I know there are con artists in those areas for sure, but there are also people in every walk of life who are con artists.

But we do not question those folks because we are familiar with them on an everyday basis. We do not think all lawyers are con artists because most of us have one that is honest, dependable, and trustworthy.

The same with doctors, etc.

I wonder how many of us know someone who has been to a medium, psychic, or a clairvoyant?

I am sure we do, but I wonder how many of us have ever asked them how it went, and could they be trusted?

We all have headsets that conform our thinking. These headsets are comfortable, and we do not dare take them off. We have grown accustomed to these headsets for most of our lives that we do not know anything else. These are headsets that our families, friends, and society has told us to put on and never take off.

We have had these headsets on for so long that sometimes we have no idea what is going on in the 'outside' world.

Because of my metaphysical gifts I run across skeptics all the time, and that is okay, because I used to be one myself. I was born that way as my analytical mind naturally pushes back on things that are not of the physical world and especially the five senses.

I have witnessed the healing effect on those who come to see me.

This would not have been possible, if I did not open my mind to more possibilities. I had to radically change the way I think about the world, the universe, religion, spirituality, etc.

So, what is the worst that could happen if you changed the way you think? About all the topics that you have a definitive opinion on. What is the concern? What is the hold up? What is the fear?

Just for one day, consider looking at things from a completely different viewpoint and see what happens. There is a whole world of new information that is waiting for you to discover.

Is it time to create your own 'bizarro world' where you see things that go opposite of what you know and were taught to be true?

This is how wisdom is obtained . . . not by the things you already know, but by discovering things that you once thought were not possible.

Let us get to this word *'metanoia'* and its meaning. Metanoia means a 'profound change of heart and mind.' To raise the veil of the world of Spirit, you will find yourself on the metanoia path as you will discover things about yourself and your life that perhaps you never knew existed.

You will meet ***beings of light*** that have strange and unusual names that are from other dimensions but are 'here' to help you.

You will encounter ***Spirit guides;*** your Spirit guides, people who have walked the earth, some of them several hundred years old who have been with you since before you were born. They are here to help guide you in your quest for more knowledge, wisdom, and the search for a better life.

You will discover ***Ascended Masters;*** men and women who have ascended to higher positions in the higher realms and dimensions who are here to help us in our time of need. Some of these masters have unusual names but they have been around for thousands of years.

You will become aware of your ***Higher Self,*** that part of you that is your essence that resides in the higher levels of consciousness.

You will realize the gift of healing and how everyone has this gift in some form or manner. Unthinkable, I know, but true. God has put all these resources at your disposal for you to use and use wisely.

You are gifted and now is the time to realize what a sacred being you are. Spend a few minutes with the meditation below and start to uncover the undiscoverable.

TAKE FIVE

Take three deep breaths and exhale slowly letting out the tensions of the day and the things that are worrying you the most. Give it up to the Universe.

Ask yourself this question:

"Am I ready for a change in my life?"

Close your eyes and contemplate what your life might look like tomorrow, that it did not look like today.

Peace.

Chapter 3

VIBRATIONS

"If you want to find the secrets of the universe,
think in terms of energy, frequency, and vibration."
—Nikola Tesla—

BLESSED ARE THE RISK TAKERS

I have a confession to make that I have made on previous occasions. I was not a particularly good student. I remember the days when we had to go back and get our report cards on the last day of school and almost everyone knew they were going to pass and move onto the next grade, except for me.

I did not study very well which means in my case, I did not read nor retain information. I did not know how to study. However, I did love pictures and images, which is why my metaphysical gift of clairvoyance is so strong.

Images speak to me . . . literal and symbolic.

In addition to not being the best student; I also did not listen to directions very well and teachers were always having to repeat to me several times the lessons of the day.

This is ironic because in addition to clairvoyance, another gift I have is **clairaudient**, which means I hear but not with my ears. It is another 'sixth sense' gift from the Universe.

Put this all together with the fact that I am an analytical person who tends to lean towards a scientific mindset when questioning things.

Therein lies the risk to the belief in things that are difficult to comprehend with the five senses.

Add to this formula that the Universe wanted me to start writing books.

Spirit saw in me a writer and deep down also saw in me the potential to listen to the Universe and become a lover of writing and a lover of books.

There is no hiding after you have written a book because you put it out there for the world to either love it, hate it, ignore it, or be indifferent towards it.

I took a risk and started writing books for people like me...who maybe are not the best readers, to make it an easy, simple read. And so, I did.

There comes a time when you must listen to the Universe. Listen to God . . . listen to Spirit . . . listen to Jesus . . . listen to a higher source such as your intuition and take a chance.

Risk . . . is it ever worth taking?

Let me see if I can answer that question.

As I mentioned previously, I am retired from a long and rewarding career in sales that paid me very well to pursue what I feel is a calling from above and from within. To help people on their path in life through the metaphysical gifts that I have been given and to put some of my messages and writings into books is pursuing the risk.

You heard me right . . . pursuing the risk.

Others must help you take a risk because we never take a risk alone. And sometimes we must go after the risk instead of waiting for it to show up on our doorstep.

When you lift the veil and peek inside the spirit world, you're taking a risk. You're going to see things and experience things that might take you by surprise. You are going to hear and feel things that might take you by surprise. If you are like me it might take time, so be patient.

There's going to be one thing that may not take you by surprise and that's the desire to go back again and go deeper inside that realm.

You're going to want to see what is on the other side.

You're going to want to hear what the Universe has to say.

You're going to want to experience firsthand what it's like to communicate with the other side because we all have that capability even though it may manifest itself differently with you than it does with me, and that's okay.

I do readings, individual, group, and on the radio, and I write books.

You may be more of a healer and heal people on your path or you may be called to go into trance, which is cool as well.

Eventually, you are going to want to know more even if it is just from a curious point of view.

That is what it's like inside the other realm where time doesn't exist, walls between religions don't exist, and where physical bodies are somewhat irrelevant meaning our sexuality isn't an issue like it is here on the earth plane.

If you look at the great discoveries in life, there were risks taken along the way as the people who made these discoveries pushed the boundaries and the borders of their conventional wisdom until they 'cracked the code' so to speak.

Religious leaders, scientists, musicians, athletes, authors, or anyone who has dared to push beyond their own veils in front of them found out what it was like when they made the choice or choices to keep going forward despite setbacks and obstacles in their paths.

These risk takers we will call the entrepreneurs of the Universe. Entrepreneurs of the Spirit.

Trust me though when I say that you might be tested time and time again because of the knowledge that you have accumulated all your life.

It might not be easy as close friends and perhaps even members of your own family will look at you and tilt their head slightly to one side as if to say . . . "WTF? You're conversing with dead people?"

You might even get tired of what you are going through and think, "I must be crazy thinking about the Universe or God or Spirit in this way."

The temptation to pull away will be great but I am telling you to exercise due diligence because it will pay off in terms of wisdom, enlightenment, and knowledge.

One last note; in this busy, noisy, tension-filled world, you will have to find a way to quiet yourself and ask the Universe to help you slow down so you can listen. When you hear nothing is when you will hear everything.

TAKE FIVE

Take a deep breath, breathing in the finger pointing
that you witnessed or were a part of today and
then breathing out all this negativity sending it
into the Universe where it will be transformed into
something positive and useful.

Ask yourself this question:

"Do I have a gift that is somewhere beyond the veil
that is waiting for me to use and if I do...what is it?"

Close your eyes and allow your Higher Self to guide
you towards that gift.

Take your time, and if nothing materializes that
is okay. It will and know that your gift got a little
closer to you during this meditation and that is a
good thing.

BUCKLE UP

Years ago, my wife and I were invited to a 'meditation circle' by our housekeeper who was a medium. We knew there would be other mediums in attendance but knew little about what to expect. Nevertheless, we were curious, so we said yes to our housekeeper's invitation. When we got there, we exchanged pleasantries and sat down amongst the dozen or so folks who were there. They seemed like nice people who you would meet in the check-out line at the grocery store. We closed our eyes after the leader had given us some instructions and as he led us through a guided meditation, I became bored. I had been through numerous guided meditations before as a leader in a Catholic leadership retreat movement and I basically despised most meditations.

I had an issue turning off my brain just to get into a state of relaxation, so I normally just closed my eyes and let my mind wander. After what seemed like an eternity, the guided and silent portion of the meditation was over and now it was time to discuss what we saw, felt, or heard. For me, I saw nothing, felt bored, and heard the icemaker of the refrigerator in the distance in the kitchen. But as we went around the room, the folks in the circle started to excitedly describe what they had experienced.

I must admit I was jealous, and I wondered, how could this be? How could all these folks experience these wondrous things and all I saw was the inside of my eyelids? Then, another curious thing happened. The leader went into a trance as a spirit, who happened to be his main spirit guide, 'possessed' his body and his face as his mannerism and his voice instantly changed.

Even though he was from Puerto Rico and spoke fluent Spanish, this was a different type of Spanish dialect and a lady in the circle translated into English what this spirit guide was telling all of us.

That evening was when I first gently **lifted the veil of the spirit world** and glanced at the other side. I was not sure what I was witnessing and must admit it took me by surprise to see this type of transfiguration happening right in front of me.

I felt uncomfortable as this spirit (I later learned about spirit guides and this was his main guide) started to talk to everyone in the circle, including my wife and me.

I had not been warned about this so yes, as Doc Brown said in *Back to The Future*, "You're going to see some serious %$@#!" This looked like serious %$@#! to me. I immediately dismissed this occurrence and thought this was not for me. And yet, my curiosity brought me back time and time again to the point that when the trance mediums started to deliver messages, it did not seem out of the ordinary.

I went to this mediumship/meditation circle every week for almost four years, as this is where my gifts were first discovered and eventually developed.

When I first pulled back the veil of the spirit world that night, it was never my intention to seek out any gifts that I had or even thought I had or to find out my purpose and mission in life.

Quite honestly, I didn't have much time in my life (or so it seemed) to think about such things and even if I did have time to think about heavy-handed subjects and topics such as those, I wouldn't even know where to begin.

I did not know much about metaphysics or mediumship or clairvoyance, I was just curious as to what it was all about. I thought that if my wife, Mary, and I went, we would meet some cool people that we could hang around with and have something to do on a Saturday night meeting them for dinner and then again something to do on Sunday evenings at the circle.

I was never into anything 'new age' and my straight as a board, structured self would never attempt to do what I found myself doing, which was pushing my boundaries out so hard that I wanted to explore more and more of the spirit realm. To say all of this was so far out of my comfort level is putting it mildly. Please keep in mind that I was in my mid-fifties when this happened. I absolutely did not need my life turned upside down, but I was about to embark on a wild ride, so wild that I forgot to buckle up.

During this time as my wife and I started going to the circle, things started to happen in our house. We have a two-story home and when we were downstairs, we started to hear noises upstairs. Knocks and bumps of all sorts started to take place. I vividly remember one such incident.

I was home alone doing my paperwork and I heard a series of footsteps going across our bedroom upstairs. I thought nothing of it as I knew it was Mary getting ready for work. Then my face froze as I realized she had already left for work.

I sat there on the couch with my laptop and probably did not move for a couple of minutes thinking, "What in the world is going on?" The noises got louder, and when we went to bed, the noises started happening all around us.

Other mediums came to our house for dinners, etc. proclaiming that there was a lot of energy and spirit in our house as the spirits felt it was a good place to hang out. After years of this happening not only when we were alone, but when others were in the house, it became so commonplace that unless it's an unusual noise or knocks upstairs, Mary and I just look at each other and then go about our business. We do cleanse the house on occasion, and before every reading that I do in my office upstairs, I sage the room with positive intentions declaring that space to be sacred space.

This is exactly what I mean by buckle up.

A journey through the pathways of the Universe calls for one to buckle up. That is the advice I can give for someone who embarks on this potentially life-changing but at the same time challenging endeavor. The reasons for me to tell you to buckle up are numerous other than what I mentioned previously.

Beyond this world that we know so well there are things that are going to make you uncomfortable and edgy as you learn more about the other side of life that you might not know so well.

You will experience what it's like to take trips without leaving your home. You will experience not only glimpses into the future but also some opportunities to revisit the past to see what can be learned from those choices that you made long ago. Depending on how far you want to go you might visit other worlds, other dimensions, and other layers of the veil. You are going to want to have to do it for it to happen.

You are going to have to reduce the noise, the drama, the activity that swirls around you daily to connect to the other side. You are going to have to desire this change in your life for it to happen. This means deciding on spending some time in silence which can be difficult and might take some getting used to.

What you will get out of visiting the other side depends upon what you put into it. Plain and simple.

TAKE FIVE

Take a deep breath and breathe in the noise around you and then breathe it out again sending it into the Universe where it will be turned into silence.

Ask yourself this question:

"If I could go anywhere in the world, or even beyond this world, just by sitting here and imagining it, where would I go?"

Close your eyes and sit back and enjoy your trip.

THE SNOW CONE EFFECT

This chapter might be challenging for some of you so just bear with me as you go through it.

It's been cool and hip for the past several years or so for people to say, "Be the best version of yourself."

It's hard for us to even know what our best version is. I would like to think that our best version of ourselves is still on the horizon. Maybe that is when we go to our Higher Self which contains our soul, our essence, our light in the higher realms of consciousness for insight and wisdom. It is the higher realms of consciousness that our Higher Selves connect to. Other theologians call it our 'true self.'

Our Higher Self may also simultaneously exist in another place . . . a parallel universe. It certainly sounds New Age-ish as most things these days are swept under the New Age carpet when we do not know where to put them. Another universe?

Sounds incredible when you think about it. Most of us when we think of an alternate version of ourselves go to *Superman* when he meets his 'other self' or 'twin' who appears to be opposite of him. Bizarro World is what I believe they called it.

Or the episode of *Seinfeld* when Elaine meets a group that is just like them but again, opposite. What if there is another universe where another version of us exists? What would that version of us do? What would that version of us be like?

What would that version of us think of us? And here is an interesting thought . . . what if that version in the other universe was aspiring to be more like us? Are they trying to be the best version of themselves so they can live up to our expectations?

Everything we do impacts everything in this universe AND the hypothetical parallel universe so why not do good deeds, have thoughts that are pure, honest, and positive, and help heal the people, places, and situations that land on our many paths in life?

The great salesman, trainer, and motivational speaker Zig Ziglar said it best when he said, "If you help enough people get what they want, they in turn will help you get what you want." A simple solution for many problems we face today. Helping others on their path in life so that they prosper and grow.

When I made the discovery and realized that we are all connected whether we like it or not, the parallel universe came into focus a little more for me. What if everything I do impacts the other universe or other dimensions? Beyond this physical world lies many dimensions in which there are a vast number of endless possibilities that keeps pushing our minds to the outer edges of reality.

Meaning, to stretch our imagination is to think of the possibility of a parallel universe. So, how do we meet it? Can we impact it by traveling to it and if we can make it to this alternate universe, what will we find?

Speaking of stretching our imagination, I want to refer to the Leonardo DiCaprio movie *Inception*, which ranks as one of my all-time favorites. If you will recall the movie features a group of men (and Ellen Page) who insert themselves into the dreams of a rich businessman who will inherit his ailing father's company when he passes in order to plant an idea so that it appears at the moment of inception. This idea will then present itself as an original thought when if used correctly will help the planet.

If we look at that movie and wonder where do original thoughts come from, is it so bizarre to think there is another version of us somewhere else? Not exactly like us, but another version of us.

Unicorns, fairies, trolls…these are things that we look at and do not think twice about because they are legends or fairy tales. Drilling down, much like the syrup on a snow cone, we can come to another assumption that the authors or the people were passing down these stories from generation to generation using their imagination. But where does it start?

Everything has some sort of beginning so when we look at things such as a parallel universe and other 'oddities' someone had to have started this conversation or story for it to take hold.

These are stories or legends that we tell our children at bedtime, but children have the most wisdom of any of us so is it a coincidence that children are the ones that embrace these stories?

As adults, we are too busy worrying about the outcome of stories such as I've described here, and too busy shooting down the realities of such nonsense because there's no such things as unicorns, right?

Children aren't beholden to the trappings and shackles of society when it comes to belief systems. They see things differently and do not think about the outcome of things. Children see things as they really are and nothing else. It's why magicians rate children as their worst audience because they do not spend time figuring the tricks out. They do not need to. They see things from a unique perspective and that is what the

Universe wants us to do. Put on the mind of a child and look at things differently.

Going back to the snow cone for a moment, I used to love snow cones as a kid. The syrup would color the top so that it would dazzle you and as you worked your way down, the syrup would become richer and richer to where you could almost drink it, especially on a hot, humid summer day. It was an awesome treat and still is today.

The innocence of a child and how he or she looks at things is like how as adults we must 'drill down' and drink the syrup of the Universe. That is the sweet spot of letting yourself go and imagining things that you once might have thought were impossible. Perhaps, now if you think of a world or dimension where another version of you exists, it might not be so farfetched.

TAKE FIVE

Take a deep breath and breathe in all the positivity that surrounds you as a person and exhale, breathing it out into the Universe so that 'your other self' or others will benefit from it.

Ask yourself this question even if you do not believe what you are about to ask:

"Is there another version of me somewhere else?"

Close your eyes, knock down the borders of your mind, and meditate on that which might have been previously unthinkable to you. Let whatever comes to you, come to you. Peace.

THE COMMUNION OF TREES

For years, I was the quintessential traveling salesperson on the road, spending nights in so many hotels and in so many different places that sometimes I couldn't even remember what city I was in and other times had trouble remembering (when morning came) if I was at my house or in a hotel. I did this for over forty years, so you have a better idea of where I am coming from.

The road was my avenue and path of prosperity for my family and me, so I trudged out every Monday or Tuesday morning and hit the road. I have calculated that I have spent close to nine and a half years of my life in a hotel room. As I write this chapter that's about fifteen percent of my life and that still does not count the nights where I came home from the road around 9 p.m. or later after the kids had already gone to bed.

During these travels, cell towers were going up left and right and, in most cases, taking the place of the pager towers that were already there. Pagers were a hot thing when my kids were in school, but cell phones were quickly taking over the communication landscape. Now for my segue.

The title of this chapter is a bit challenging as when I sat down and came up with the title it simply did not make sense to me. As an author, I always start with the title, and then sit back and see what energy comes from it. Then I start writing and inevitably it all starts to fall into place. But this title became more confusing to me the more I looked at it. I even contemplated changing the title but the Universe calmed my concerns and put it all together.

I have never considered myself much of a tree-hugger, although I love being outside and in nature. It is the quietness and the sanctuary of the woods, forest, or even my backyard that just leaves me with a tranquil and peaceful feeling. It separates me from the noise that seems to take up all the space in my life.

As I progressed further and further into the realm of spirit, it directed my attention to more and more things that I seemed to have taken for granted . . . like trees. The more I pushed forward as I lifted the veil, the more Spirit navigated me back to the earth plane to explore and get closer to nature.

Nature is certainly a way of appreciating God's beauty and sacred touch. Nature is God's way of surrounding us with His presence as a reminder of how loved we all are. Looking at all the natural sacredness around us does lift one's spirits when we are going through tough, difficult, and trying times. I have often loved the sound of rain; it is nature's way of chanting. It is no wonder that when it rains we almost instantly want to go take a nap or just find a place to relax.

That is where my journey of discovering trees has taken me. A fellow medium told me that trees would help raise my vibrations and therefore assist me not only in obtaining more knowledge and wisdom but also aid me in my ongoing development of my gifts. She suggested talking to the trees by thanking them for their wisdom and beauty.

I know what you are thinking (because of my gifts no doubt) that "Jerry has gone a bit too far in all of this love nature and hug-a-tree mindset."

You could very well be right, but when I tell you that it has made a difference just by noticing the trees and mentally talking to them while on my daily walks. I am convinced more than ever that my friend was right.

I do believe that trees talk to each other and talk to us as well. I can almost hear them communicating to each other as I pass them while walking. I can hear them whispering and I swear on more than one occasion, I see them moving as I go by whereas they were not moving before.

Trees are alive with so much energy that the Irish have written about the oak tree being a portal for not only the druids but the Spirit realm as well. I believe they are on to something.

Trees do participate in a communion of sorts as they partake in the lifeblood of everything around them, including us. They are everywhere and yet we go about our daily lives never noticing them. Perhaps if we think of them this way, it might make them more noticeable . . . trees, nature's version of a cell tower.

TAKE FIVE

This is more of an exercise than a meditation.

No matter where you are, go outside and hang around a tree for a few minutes, even if it is just sitting on a park bench. Appreciate the beauty and splendor of one of God's most magnificent creations.

Doing this repeatedly will boost your connection to the Universe. If you want to meditate near a tree, that is even better . . . just close your eyes and sit back and give thanks to the trees for their grace, or their shade, and for always being there.

WHAT HAPPENS AT 3 A.M.?

What happens in between the hours of 3 a.m. and 4 a.m.?

There are numerous explanations but there is one that gives the best and most reasonable explanation and the one that Spirit has wanted me to pass on.

In this book and during my speeches and lectures and writings, there is much discussion about the veil that lies between the physical world and the non-physical world.

The Irish call it the Thin Veil and this veil is supposedly at its thinnest around 3 a.m.

What does this mean to you and me?

It can mean several things, but the one thing I want to focus on might make more sense and have more meaning to most folks reading this.

Think of our body, mind, and spirit as a computer that has all the components that an actual computer has. Hard drives, screens, keyboards, etc.

Just like our real computers, our mind, body, spirit computer needs rest and that's where sleep comes in. Our computers cannot be on 24/7 and neither can our mind, body, and spirit.

And just like our real computers, occasionally our mind, body, and spirit needs upgrades and improvements and that's where downloads happen.

When we set up downloads we normally look for a good connection so the download is accurate and hopefully fast.

Think of the veil at its thinnest as a prime opportunity for a good connection for downloads to happen. These downloads are crucial to our development.

These downloads also come at a time when you are the most vulnerable because of the veil being so thin and at a time when your borders and filters are down.

When we sleep our borders go down and anything and anybody can come in, in terms of energies and spirits, both positive and negative.

It's like the movie *Jurassic Park* when the electric fences are turned off and the T-Rex comes charging through.

In addition to downloads from the Universe, spirits can also roam around in your house as they see the veil thinning, and depending upon whether they are positive or negative can decide to come through and either make it a good or not so good experience.

Which is why sometimes we wake up around 3 a.m..

It is (to use yet another movie reference) like in *Star Wars* when Obi-Wan Kenobe feels a disturbance in the force. Sometimes we feel a thinning of the veil through Spirit activity and wake up.

Other times we do not wake up at 3 a.m. and wake up at our normal time and have a massive headache and we do not know why.

I just call it download overload where too much information, etc. from the Spirit world has been downloaded to you and that abundance has created a headache.

Simply say before you go to bed, "Spirit; easy on the downloads."

How can we ensure that the thinning veil doesn't impact us in a negative way?

Prayers of protection.

What will enhance this opportunity for the Universe to download information to you are prayers of protection that you can say before you go to sleep.

Perhaps it is always a good idea to say our prayers at night. To give thanks for our blessings, talk to those loved ones who have passed and tell them how much we miss them, and most of all say a prayer of protection.

I begin the day and end the day with a prayer of protection. I give thanks for my gifts and my blessings in life and ask to be protected by the light of God, the infinite, and divine and to ensure no negative entities, energies, or spirits come into the light.

This ensures I have protection in my dreams and allows the downloads that the Universe is giving me.

Loved ones want to reach out and tell us that they are okay, and it is when they have enough light or when the veil is thin that they reach out.

Embrace the other side for they have much to teach us in the way of the Universe and much to download so we can experience this for ourselves.

TAKE FIVE

Take three deep breaths and then exhale all the drama of the day giving it up and putting it in the hands of God.

Close your eyes and just be in the present moment and ask for protection from negative entities, energies, and spirits.

Peace.

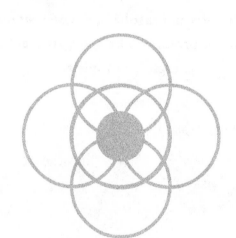

Chapter 4

ENERGY

"We are all connected; To each other, biologically.
To the earth, chemically. To the rest of the universe atomically."

—Neil DeGrasse Tyson—

BLACK MATTER LIVES

Black . . . the color that seems to represent darkness, evil, negativity, vampires, witches, cats, etc. is probably one of the most misunderstood colors and here is why.

In the movies, bad cowboys and villains were identified as wearing something black, especially hats.

However, the people who historically have worn black do not see it that way at all.

Johnny Cash wore black, not only because he liked the color, but because it rebelled against what he saw as injustices in the world, which was the poor, the homeless, the men and women who were in prison that had paid their dues but were left there anyway, etc.

At funerals, we wear black to pay respect for those loved ones we have lost and to mourn.

Priests wear black to represent the suffering in the world, especially the suffering of Jesus.

I was taught in elementary school that white was the presence of all color and black was the absence of all color . . . ironic isn't it that black was the absence of all color, but for generations we were determined to call all people who were black, 'colored folks.'

How do black people or people of color feel? I never thought much about it until I attended a conference in New Mexico one year and heard from several impressive speakers who happen to be black how they grew up with this stigma attached to them. How they have heard all their lives that white is good and black is bad.

Black . . . nighttime is black, but at nighttime is when we get our rest. Nighttime is when most of us talk to God. Nighttime is when we spend time with our families; a healing time for most of us. Nighttime is when we can decompress from the busy world and give thanks for all the blessings we have been given. Nighttime is when our bodies heal themselves.

Nighttime is when we look up and see things that we could not see in the daytime.

It's ironic that in several of the mediumship circles I've been involved in I've been told not to wear black because it's offensive, but then the very next thing that happens is we dim the lights and are plunged into darkness before we meditate.

Back in the day, black light posters were big sellers. I had several in my bedroom growing up and, of course, had my trusty black light to illuminate them and add color to my room.

It was the black light that illuminated these posters and made them stand out and come alive showing me things that I could not see. You can see the analogy.

As I write this the Black Lives Matter movement is visible and growing every day, making people aware of the plight and the suffering that black people face every day.

I did not fully understand this issue because I am Caucasian,

I used to be critical of this movement, insisting that the All Lives Matter movement was the more appropriate way of addressing this issue.

Then one day Spirit told me what this movement was all about. Spirit showed me that to sweep the issue of black people being persecuted and discriminated against under the rug of 'all lives' was deemphasizing the issues that they face.

Spirit said that it's like when someone says "cancer sucks" and I say "all illnesses suck" putting cancer in the same category as the common cold.

I am deemphasizing the need to draw attention to cancer much like the need to draw attention to the issues that black people face.

I understand that now.

And then there's dark matter which is believed to make up twenty-seven percent of the Universe.

Some say dark matter is simply nothing, but we have given it a name. So, it must be something even if we cannot define it and put it in a file that we can label and understand.

Scientists cannot adequately offer definitions of what it could be, but let's pretend for a moment that it is the Universe challenging us to look at those things that we deem indefinable from a spiritual and metaphysical view and not strictly from a scientific view.

Maybe it also serves to get us to try to look at things differently much like BLACK LIVES MATTER.

What I have learned from the Universe is that the light within each one of us is what makes us special. I have heard from beings of light that dwell on the other side in higher dimensions that our planet needs to heal and not look at ways that divide us but look at ways that can bring us closer together. The energy of the planet needs to be positive, not negative energy.

It is why children are so precious and loving. Their innocence towards other children who look different than they are is something to emulate and integrate into our own lives. It is a model for peace on this planet.

Children do not see different colors, they just see little ones their age who just want to play, and they think that is awesome.

The planet we live on needs to recapture some of that innocence in order to heal. When that innocence starts to occur, discriminations and prejudices will not be the rule of the day, but the exception. The only way we as a society can heal is to come to the realization that our souls, the very essence of our being, existed long before it occupied the body we now have and that it never began as one color.

We are made in the image of the creator, and the Divine One does not limit himself, herself, or itself to one race, one religion, or one ethnic group.

The fingerprint of God is within each one of us, and that alone should inspire all of us to do better and treat one another as equals because we are.

In William Paul Young's beautiful book, *The Shack*, loved ones in the afterlife are shown as figures or beams of different colors and shades of light.

Contained in these beams of light is energy.

Depending upon how high one has passed, evolved, or ascended determines the focus and brightness of the light.

Tragic circumstances such as suicides, murders, addictions, overdoses, abusive behavior, etc. will take longer for that individual to find the necessary energy and light to ascend.

There will be lessons to learn in that regard.

There is no need for diversity in the afterlife because there is no need for that word.

The reason there is no need for that word is because everyone in the afterlife eventually finds light and are treated with love. We were all born into this life and other lives touched by the Divine.

Are you willing to take a risk by recognizing the light that dwells within those that are different than us? That is where true healing starts.

TAKE FIVE

Take a deep breath and breathe in all of the prejudices that you believe you have toward one person that you know. Now exhale, let it out, and send it back to the Universe for healing, acknowledging in your own way, that prejudices do not own you anymore.

Ask yourself this question:

"Is it time to forgive myself because I'm not perfect?"

Now close your eyes and meditate on this for as long as you want, realizing that you are as sacred as anyone that has ever been on this planet.

LIVING ON THE FAULT LINE

In addition to loving jazz, I absolutely love classic rock.

Could be that I used to play drums for a very short time in my life and tried to learn my favorite songs or it could just be that classic rock takes me back to my high school years which for me were the best.

My buddies and I used to usher for rock concerts, and even though we didn't get paid, we got to sit backstage and watch the best groups in the world for free.

I remember one time we actually got to sit on stage off to the side and watch 'that little ole' band from Texas named ZZ Top.

This of course was back when they were clean cut and wore ten-gallon hats, long before the beards and MTV. Anyway, this brings me to one of my all-time favorite bands, The Doobie Brothers.

I have always loved The Doobie Brothers, pre and post Michael McDonald.

That music was a magical time in my life (the early seventies) and it helped define my happiness (along with marijuana, sorry). Back to the music.

The Doobie Brothers' "Livin' on the Fault Line" is one of my favorite albums, back of course, when there were albums.

The album produced no major hits, but critics argue that this is the most compelling and musically challenging album of The Doobie Brothers' career.

Despite the lead singer leaving the band early in the making of the album, others stepped up their game to produce an enlightening jazz fusion, R&B influenced album, especially the title track.

The title track starts out as one thing, then changes course, then goes in an entirely different direction. Let's face it, it's not every day that a classic rock song contains a xylophone solo, but somehow, they make everything fit together and work and produce an amazing sound.

Critics argue that this album, often overlooked by diehard Doobie fans, deserves a second look.

As I am writing this, it is now 2020 and we are looking forward, but does that mean we shouldn't look back at 2019 and see what we've learned, if anything?

It could be that it wasn't the best of years; no hits, but compelling, challenging, and in many ways a critical success?

Does last year deserve a second look?

Did last year go in a million different directions but somehow you made it work and you're still here?

It's amazing that every year on New Year's Eve it never fails that someone will talk about how horrible the year was for the twelfth year in a row.

Why is that?

Have we programmed ourselves year after year to focus on the assumption that the previous year was the worst only to be outdone by the current year?

There are bad years and there are good years.

And this past year there have been losses of loved ones and heartaches and financial challenges, etc. But I'm still here and so are you.

Time to acknowledge the successes and challenges of the previous year so we can apply those learnings to the year that we now find ourselves in.

Speaking of fault lines, do you ever feel the earth shift underneath your feet? Okay that was metaphorically speaking so let's put it another way, do you ever feel uncomfortable for no apparent reason?

You feel on edge, but you cannot explain why. You go around and feel as if you have forgotten something or somebody, but you have not.

You have a desire to be alone or want silence in your life. Something just seems off or different, either about you or the people around you.

Okay, so it's not the earth shifting, but something sure is shifting and that something is you.

What is it?

This shift could very well be a shift in consciousness. According to experts, there are several levels of consciousness, each level bringing an increased awareness and intensity.

In his book, *The Universal Christ*, the acclaimed author, Franciscan priest, and mystic Richard Rohr calls our consciousness our 'inner mirror.'

According to the website *Ananda*, the three main levels are subconscious, conscious, and superconscious.

Subconscious is the 'stuff in which dreams are made.'

Conscious is the rational awareness that usually guides our decisions.

Superconscious is where intuition and heightened mental clarity flow.

It is in this superconscious arena that we experience the spirit realm simply because the superconscious allows borders, barriers, and limitations to melt away leaving things that the conscious state pushes back on.

This uneasiness could also be a shift in your spirit guides, meaning one spirit guide is pulling back and another one is coming to the forefront for this chapter of your life. We have multiple spirit guides and they stay with us all of our lives, but at certain times, much like a tag team, one may pull back and another one may step up to assist you, especially if you're about to enter the second half of your life.

The second half of your life is where you seek more wisdom and knowledge in your purpose and mission in life.

The famed psychiatrist Carl Jung talked about the second half of life as a self-realization that one has whether it is religion or taking stock of one's life.

Richard Rohr talks about the second half of life as a part of our life, regardless of age, whereby those of us who have fallen can understand 'up' and the journey upwards.

Where does this come from? Where does this desire for possible self-transformation come from?

Could it be that this is a desire to lift the veil of a world that you know extraordinarily little about and see what is beyond the physical realm?

It is a desire to want to know more about your life, who you are, and what your purpose in life is currently and what it might look like in the future.

This shifting could also be telling you to get moving and go towards that veil.

When there is an earthquake, the fault lines shift, and we must get moving to avoid falling into the earth's core.

The minute you stop asking questions is the minute you stop yearning for more.

TAKE FIVE

Take a deep breath and breathe in any questions you have about what is beyond the physical world and breathe out all those questions so Spirit can turn them into answers.

Then ask this question, not of yourself, but of Spirit:

"Can you show me a glimpse of what is beyond the veil?"

Close your eyes and relax and clear your mind as best as you can and allow anything that comes, no matter what.

LEARN, GROW, EVOLVE

I discovered the other side of the veil by sitting in a meditation/mediumship circle every week for almost four years. It was an uplifting and extremely spiritual experience that I would highly recommend to everybody. At times though, I felt like I was being left behind by the Universe while most everyone else was on a fast track to knowledge, wisdom, and intelligence. It was extremely frustrating, especially because I wanted to know what everyone else knew. I wanted to hear what everyone else was hearing. I wanted to see and experience what everyone else was seeing and experiencing.

I kept hearing a voice that said patience, patience, patience. In my typical 'get it done today' fashion, I would send back a response to that voice indicating that I did not have time to be patient, which is a somewhat convoluted statement to say the least. The frustrations kept building until one day it hit me what the Universe was trying to teach me. A lesson that was not easy for someone who is wired analytically like me.

I learned the hard way that much like dreams, messages from the Universe come to us in fragments or pieces. The engineer, in this case being God, wants us to figure some of this stuff out. In one sense, God is teaching us how to fish so we do not just show up and buy fish or depend upon someone to provide fish for us. This is all done so we can move forward in our lives with a sense of how to connect to Spirit, how to look at the world around us and pick up signs and messages, and how to interpret those messages and use them in our daily lives.

When our loved ones pass, they will attempt to contact us in a multitude of ways.

It takes a lot of energy for us to connect with the other side.

It could be that they will appear in our dreams to say things that were left unsaid. I know some of my clients get frustrated because a loved one of a friend has appeared in their dreams but my client has not experienced any of their loved ones coming through in their dreams.

I tell them patience is needed and it could be that my clients loved ones are manifesting themselves in different and unique ways. I know as I am writing this book, I have just lost my brother to cancer at the age of sixty-six. This means that all the members of my family passed in their sixties. After my brother passed, I started seeing hawks where I didn't see them before and about two hours ago, as I'm writing this chapter, a beautiful hawk flew into our backyard and perched on an old bench that we have had for years.

I know that is a sign from my brother, Stan. Some people see their loved ones who have passed in their bedroom late at night to give them comfort. Others feel them nearby or smell a cigar or pipe that their grandfather used to smoke.

These are all messages and signs from our loved ones as a way of giving us comfort and helping us on our path that we are on. They are in a much better place to help us, believe it or not.

Sometimes it is not our loved ones who are reaching out; sometimes it's Spirit or the Universe giving us clarity and direction to assist us as we move forward with our lives. It is all about energy.

All the above are pieces of a much larger puzzle that we will use on the path that we are all currently on. The spirit world has much to teach us, but they must feed the information to us one morsel at a time as we have limitations to how much we can take in.

It's not a step by step process, especially when someone is teaching us about the other side or giving us a reading or just relaying what they're picking up from Spirit.

It tends to go like this and for those who are analytical, I've put the morsels of knowledge in steps basically contradicting myself.

STEP ONE—Receive a message from beyond the veil.

STEP TWO—**Learn** what that message means.

STEP THREE—Receive another message from beyond the veil.

STEP FOUR—**Grow** with what you've learned from previous messages.

STEP FIVE—Receive another message from beyond the veil.

STEP SIX—**Evolve** by applying the learning and growing that you've done with the messages you've received into your mission and purpose in life.

During my time in the weekly meditation circle, we would occasionally practice giving messages to each other. I vividly remember one such reading that I received. It was from a friend named Eric and after the group meditated, we broke up into partners and Eric was my message or reading partner.

He told me that there was a woman and a man from the world of spirit who were telling me that they were surprised that I was 'into' the gifts of mediumship and clairvoyance, etc.

They felt that I had been given everything on earth over the past twenty years or so that would supply me with the answers to all my questions regarding religion and spirituality. I had no idea or the slightest clue who in the world these two people were.

Thinking that the entire message/reading would make perfect sense to me as it stood on its own was a lesson that I had to learn so it would help me on my path. It was not until a year after telling everyone who would listen that sometimes we're not meant to hear the entire message from Spirit, that I would figure out who the man and the woman were that came through.

They were my brother's in-laws who were both Methodist ministers (as was my brother before he retired after thirty-five years) that ran the church that I somewhat grew up in. Lesson learned after a year of finally listening to my own advice and counsel.

Pieces of a message, pieces of a reading, pieces of a dream. Take the messages that the Universe is giving you, write them down, and start to process what God is telling you. He would not waste your time with useless babble He has a plan for you. Learn, Grow, and Evolve could become a way of life for you and when that happens you are going to want to know more. Most of the writings in this book and in my first book, *Channeling the Mothership: Messages from the Universe*, were exactly the 'method' that I described earlier.

Thoughts and cryptic messages from beyond the veil that standing alone did not make sense, but when I put it down and formulated the basis of a chapter or book, it all came together.

Even when I get images, I try to remember them and write them down because I know they are coming from a much higher source than me. These are thoughts and images and when pieced together form a sacred mural of what God wants you to do or perhaps what He knows can possibly aspire you to be. The random thoughts that you get daily mean something and only you can interpret them because only you have received them. Everything means something.

TAKE FIVE

Take a deep breath and breathe in the goodness that surrounds you and breathe out this same goodness so the Universe can spread your positive energy to others who need it.

Ask the Universe this question:

"Can you show me an image that I can meditate on?"

Then close your eyes, relax, and forego any preconceived notions or memories of what YOU want to see and see only what Spirit wants to show you, even if it's just darkness, because that's okay too. This darkness will eventually change; trust me on this. This might take some time, so patience is a virtue, and remember to bring your energy to the meditation.

WHO ARE YOU REALLY?

When I was growing up, my family did not have a whole lot of money as my father was a factory worker and mom was a stay-at-home mom who never learned to drive.

Back in those days, empty soda bottles could be returned for deposit money, so we scrounged everywhere we could to find coke bottles, etc. to return for money. I recall one day we were all driving home, and we spotted some empty coke bottles across a busy street with cars whizzing by.

My dad pulled over and I started to get out to go grab the bottles. On this street, which was in front of the school that I went to, I stood by the car, looked to the left and then looked to the right to make sure no cars were coming and took a step into the street. At about that time, my mom screamed, "Jerry!" and I froze as a car went right by me, so close to me that my loosely worn shirt almost hit the car's door handle. I had no idea where the car came from, but what I do know is that I was almost killed.

Which begs the question, how many lives do we have? Is the life we are currently living our only life? I never really thought about that question much. In fact, I never thought about that question at all. That is, until I started to meet people from not only the world of Spirit but also people here in the physical realm who talked about other lives.

I had heard the phrase 'old soul' but never knew what it meant other than a person who appeared to be older in knowledge and wiser in wisdom than they were in age. I never realized that it had everything to do with previous lives.

The whole reincarnation thing or living many lives thing just did not make sense to me, especially to my analytical brain that I relied upon to make sense of most things that I came across.

Some curious things, however, were starting to come to my attention that made me rethink this past life thing, as I use to refer to it as. As I became more and more interested in mediumship, I had three readings from three different mediums who did not know each other who presented me with something that even my analytical brain sat up and paid attention to.

These three mediums told me that my wife was a man in one of her previous lives. What are the chances of that happening? Three mediums who did not know each other and who gave me readings and messages at different times spread out months and months apart tell me the same thing.

I am sorry but those are things that I simply could not ignore. So, I decided to do what is commonly referred to as a 'past life regression' whereby a licensed hypnotherapist puts you into a hypnotic state and takes you back where you can examine a past life or two to see how it impacts the life that you're currently living. The amazing thing I learned is that at the age of twelve, I was tragically killed in two different previous lives. Once in Nazi occupied Poland, and the other one during a festival in a Spanish or Mexican town.

Back to my story on the coke bottles in which I was almost struck by a car and killed. How does that story figure into a past life story? Well, you see, I was twelve when I was almost hit by that car and killed.

Unbeknownst to Diane, who wrote the foreword of this book and is the one who performed my past life regression, I had almost the same experience at the same age twelve except this time, I broke that trend or thread and survived.

I know now that I have lived several past lives and so have you. We've all experienced déjà vu where we stop for a moment and wonder why a situation or a group of people or a conversation around us suddenly seems so familiar. We even mutter to ourselves, "I've been here before in this exact spot with people saying the exact same things." It does not make sense at the time, and so we just dismiss it as something odd that has just happened.

History repeating itself? Doubt it, but what I do not doubt is that it is your past life(s) coming through. You and I are more than just this life. And these lives influence our decisions and thinking up to a certain point.

Next time you encounter a situation where everything suddenly seems familiar, just ask yourself, "I wonder what my old self did?"

Then stand back and see what your current self will now do because that will influence your future life and your future self.

TAKE FIVE

Take a deep breath and hold it for a second and then let it go slowly. Think about this thought for a moment:

"If I did have a past life, I wonder what my old self did in that life?"

Now close your eyes and slowly try to visualize yourself in another lifetime.

Do this for five minutes and just let yourself go with zero expectations on what you might experience . . . if you do not experience anything that's okay because that's an experience.

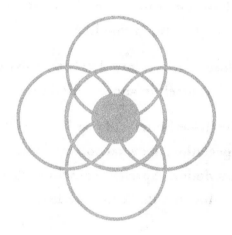

Chapter 5

RELIGION

"Let your religion be less of a theory and more of a love affair."
—Gilbert K. Chesterton—

God, Universe, Spirit

I remember the day when a woman and her husband came to see me for a couples reading. They were nice and open to what Spirit was telling them except for one small item.

Spirit kept telling the husband about his heart and that he should get it checked out. What made this seem unusual was that they were headed to Tennessee for cancer surgery for him, not heart surgery. Spirit kept pointing to the chest indicating that he needed to get it checked out. They kept insisting, very nicely, that there was nothing wrong with his heart. The woman was looking at me somewhat puzzled as if there was something wrong and I just kept telling her to make sure he got his heart checked out.

I then told them about the episode that I witnessed on Tyler Henry's TV show. Tyler Henry is known as the Hollywood Medium and I have always been extremely impressed with his mediumship and clairvoyant abilities.

On this episode, Tyler is doing a reading with Alan Thicke, a famous actor, director, and producer from Canada, and he mentions to Alan about getting his heart checked out. Tyler senses something is not right with Alan's heart.

Alan does not heed Tyler's warning from Spirit and a few weeks later he dies of a heart attack while playing sports. The couple listened intently to the story, thanked me, and took all the notes that they had written and left. I should mention here that men are stubborn (and I should know as I am one) when it comes to taking care of their health and going to the doctor.

Alan was no different than anyone that I have given readings to regarding men going to get a checkup. A few months later, the couple came back for another reading. They were sitting there looking at me and smiling. Not remembering what I had said at the previous reading, I asked what the smiles were all about.

They told me that they had gone to Tennessee for the cancer surgery, but the husband was starting to have chest pains and they checked him in at a nearby hospital. Later that night, he had triple bypass surgery as two of the arteries were one hundred percent blocked. Spirit was spot on and his life was saved.

They thanked me over and over, but I told them that it was not me. It was GUS. God, Universe, and Spirit. I allowed the metaphysical trinity that I call GUS to use me to help someone. How does a retired sales and account manager from Orlando, Florida successfully diagnose a medical condition?

The answer is easy. First, I do not diagnose anything. Spirit has been pushing me to scan people to see what might be any medical or health issues and then relay that information to the person receiving the reading. That is why I'm listed as a medical intuitive. Second, my career and what I did for a living for over thirty years had no bearing on my gifts from God. Third, I can only suggest to someone that this is what I am feeling or seeing or getting from the Universe; nothing more.

The rest is up to the person receiving the message and that is the free will that God gives us.

There is an endless supply of knowledge and wisdom on the other side of the veil waiting for us to tap into. If only we would take the time to do so.

God is the creator of all things, past, present, and future. The Universe to me is like the Christ Consciousness that lives and breathes inside each one of us, regardless if we are Christian or not. Christ Consciousness listens to everything we do and speak and think and gives us guidance, direction, and clarity. Spirit, or to some Holy Spirit, is the energy that moves throughout everything.

A book that helped me look at Christ as truly something universal is the book *The Universal Christ* by Richard Rohr. This book transcends religion so please give it a look.

God, Universe, and Spirit are one and the same which is why I use them interchangeably and all indications are they do not mind. God is not a man nor a woman. God is a bright indescribable shape of light and love that permeates through everything that has ever existed and that ever will.

Who knows what medical breakthroughs await us? Could the cure for cancer be somewhere in the Spirit realm? The knowledge that is there for the taking is within us if we only will take the time to quiet ourselves and listen.

TAKE FIVE

Take one deep breath, pulling in any questions regarding your path in life. Now, exhale, pushing out those questions and sending them to the Universe for clarity and direction.

Ask yourself this question:

"Where am I on my path for peace and happiness?"

Close your eyes and listen.

SACREDNESS OF YOU

I never thought much about me or others being a 'sacred being.' In fact, I never thought about the word 'sacred' other than how it applied to religious organizations and church. The word sacred carries with it an almost deity connotation, something that is untouchable such as a religious relic or text.

We live our lives on a daily basis, going through the motions of providing revenue for ourselves and our families. We work, have some recreational time, do some traveling along the way. Maybe we make a few major purchases and if we're parents, we watch our kids and grandkids grow up.

There is nothing about what I just described that remotely sounds like anything sacred. At least not to me. But during my journey into the realm of Spirit I started to discover some things that turned my world upside down. I started to focus on who or what 'made' us and why we were 'made.' If we believe that we are made in the image and likeness of our creator, then does not it make sense that none of us are meant to live a mundane life?

There is nothing wrong with the scenario that I described above, nothing wrong with it at all. As long as we realize that we are something special and that we're all called to project that special light around us that God created in order for others so they can realize that they are something special too.

What Spirit brought to me late one night as I was almost asleep was a sacredness flow chart and it goes something like this:

Positive thoughts = words / deeds = action = change = enlightenment = ascension = light / vibrations = energy = more positive thoughts.

Makes one think about things a little differently, doesn't it? In the end, positive thoughts come back to you full circle so that this flow continues to evolve in the Universe.

If you were to fast track this chart it would simply say thoughts = energy. One thing to keep in mind about this sacredness flow chart is that I presented it on an assumption that the thoughts were positive. If your thoughts were on a more negative scale, the flow chart would look something like this:

Negative thoughts = words / deeds = action = change = consequences= descension = darkness = lower vibrations = negative energy = more negative thoughts.

The way for us to remain a sacred being is for us to think as many positive thoughts as possible. This is difficult simply because we're trained to focus on the negative.

Scientists and researchers say that there are seven basic human emotions.

Sadness, anger, contempt, disgust, fear, joy, and surprise.

As you can plainly see, five of the seven emotions are on the negative side. To get away from the negativity in our lives there is some work to be done. We must go about rewiring our hardware and that will take some doing.

Richard Rohr, in his book *The Universal Christ* (pg. 63), says, "Brain studies have shown that we may be hardwired to focus on the problem at the expense of a positive vision." I could not have said it better myself.

Here are three ways to maintain this 'sacredness' that we're all called to evolve into.

- **CUT OFF TOXIC RELATIONSHIPS**—Nothing says negativity better than toxic relationships. Is it time to rid yourself of these relationships that do not serve you any purpose other than to feed rumors, jealously, bad feelings, etc.? If nothing else, start to put some distance between yourself and these people who do nothing but act like 'psychic vampires' as they suck and drain the life out of you.

- **SLOW DOWN ON TV**—As I write this in the year 2020 there are more than 300 reality shows that at most highlight the negative and the destructive side in people. Yes, there are exceptions, but I would guess that no more than 5-7% of these shows highlight things that are positive.

  Unfortunately, it is like a bad car wreck that we just cannot keep our eyes off. The more we watch, the more we are drawn into their world of illusion and toxicity.

- **BE PART OF YOUR SOUL'S JOURNEY**—Ask your soul, your intuition, your higher self, your essence, "Where do you want to go today?" Talk to your Spirit guide and see how this sacredness can be developed and built upon.

I called on an account that featured one of the best businessmen I have ever had the pleasure to run across. We will call him Steve. He was my main contact and for fifteen years I called on him 1-2 times a month.

Today, Steve remains a close friend. One day, as I was presenting some plans and remedies and solutions for certain products we were pitching, Steve said the following:

"Jerry, you've created a solution for which there was no problem." A brilliant statement and one that I have repeated many times in my life. I was creating solutions for problems that did not exist . . . unreal.

Why was I doing that? If you go back to what Richard Rohr said, it makes perfect sense. For my negative side to thrive and grow, I had to develop a solution just so I could identify and discuss an issue, even if it did not exist.

Hard to be sacred when your focus is on a problem.

If we decide to focus on the positive side of things, some of those desires that we have dreamt of and wished for might start to take place. That is true sacredness at its best.

TAKE FIVE

Take a deep breath, and along with it a positive thought that you currently have, then exhale and breathe out that thought so that others may benefit from the sacredness of it, as the Universe blesses it.

Focus on that positive thought and close your eyes and repeat that thought in your head, much like a mantra or a chant.

Do this repeatedly and your energy will expand and grow into something beautiful.

THE GRAND SCHEME

When we look at the Universe, or better yet our universes from an intimate point of view, it might look something like with ourselves first and then working our way down.

- OURSELVES
- OUR HOUSE
- OUR COUNTY
- OUR STATE
- OUR COUNTRY
- OUR PLANET

- OUR FAMILY
- OUR NEIGHBORHOOD
- OUR CITY
- OUR REGION
- OUR ANCESTORS
- OUR UNIVERSE

Most of the time we start with our own small universes and then branch out further and further from the center, which is our soul, our Higher Self, and see how all of that applies to the bigger picture, which is the overall Universe.

What if we turned this on its head and initiated our own paradigm shift where we literally started from zero? What if we started with the Universe and then worked our way down into our individual universes?

To see not how things apply to the Universe but to see how the Universe applies things to our own environments. This could also be your version of the big bang. All our lives we often have heard of 'the grand scheme' of things when someone is trying to tell us to look at the bigger picture.

The 'grand scheme' . . . the 30,000-foot view; the view from on high, Mount Olympus—you get the idea.

What if the grand scheme was inside us all along? One of the many themes, or schemes if you will, of this book is where do we stand on the Universe? The more I talked to those on the other side the more I was told that it is not what we think.

Instead of looking out so far into the distance and looking at the Universe from a telescope, take the opposite approach and look at the Universe from under a microscope by breaking it down into small pieces or fragments or universes.

Work backwards so to speak.

As I was writing this, Spirit told me to put down the words 'soul of the Universe.' I had never thought of those words in that way, so I went online to see what else I could find on the 'soul of the Universe.' Believe it or not, ninety percent of the things I saw put the Universe into a physical perspective as if the Universe is just planets, stars, solar systems, etc.

What if you were 'the grand scheme'? What if the 'soul of the Universe' lived inside you and everything you do? What is the soul of the Universe and how does it work?

Question: what is bigger than you? Answer: nothing. Nothing is bigger than you. This is mind-blowing because we have learned all our lives that we were just one small peg in an endless number of massive pegboards composed of an infinite number of pegs.

I hate to quote the Bible because the Bible, in my humble opinion, was never meant to be the decider of arguments or the inventor of arguments, but as a document of faith, inspiration, and beliefs. As our current Pope would say to never quote text without context. But what the heck so here goes.

Hebrew 11:3 says . . .

By faith we understand that the universe was created by the word of God, so that what is seen was *not made from things that are visible*.

"What is seen was not made out of things that are visible."

You can interpret it any way you want it, but here's my interpretation: the Universe is not just a visible quantifiable materialistic body of substance that can be defined by what we see or what we have learned from science books or in lectures, etc.

If we believe we are made in the image of the creator, then how can we not think that we are the center or the soul of the creator's Universe? The realm of spirit has made it clear how important we are in the grand scheme of things because, at the end of the day, we are the grand scheme. What can we do to ensure that we know and recognize that we are the center and the soul of the Universe?

Tell the creator, "Possess me in the most humanly way possible by your divine presence." You will have to admit that is a prayer worthy of any Universe.

The kind of possession we are talking about is not mind control or anything of that nature. We are asking for divine love to enter our very essence and being and that is all God wants from us. That is the invitation that God has been waiting for and if you have sent that invitation to God then by all means feel free to send it again, and again, and again. God will never tire of this, ever.

TAKE FIVE

Take a deep breath and exhale giving thanks to God for everything. Ask God to "possess me in the most humanly way possible by your divine presence."

Then close your eyes and absorb the love of the divine.

Which Way is Purgatory?

It is a difficult thing sitting across from someone who has lost a loved one due to suicide. For the better part of the past ten months, I have sat with someone virtually every week who has been personally affected by suicide. It is an unbelievably tragic death in which there are a thousand hard questions but zero easy answers.

There is guilt, shame, anger, bitterness, sadness, contempt, surprise, disgust...you name it; the people who have lost loved ones have probably gone through it. Virtually every human emotion possible with the lone exception of joy or happiness (and there are some who do experience those emotions depending upon the circumstance) is experienced by people who have lost a loved one due to suicide.

There are also those people who remain steadfast in believing that people who do go through with this act are doomed to an eternity in Hell. They will never be 'allowed' inside the privileged gated community called Heaven.

And the reason I say privileged (it bears repeating) is because it's apparent to me that a great deal of people who call themselves Christians (of which I'm one) go around and flaunt the fact that, "I'm going to Heaven and you're not" from an almost arrogant point of view. "I'm better than you, because I'm a Christian" seems to be the daily message that some spout. Of course this means that Jews, Muslims, Buddhists, Hindus, perhaps the entire Native American nation, etc. will never make it to Heaven.

I find that extremely hard to believe. This means that approximately four thousand religions in the world are not going to Heaven unless you happen to follow Christianity.

And of course, there are those who say that being Catholic is not exactly being Christian because we do not bring Bibles into church. We pray to saints and we have statues in our sanctuaries. Since we don't quote scripture as much as they would like us to, we may end up in Heaven but not in as nice of the houses traditional Christians such as those in the more mainstream protestant religions will occupy. We might get into Heaven because, after all, Peter was the first Pope of the Catholic Church, so we know the doorman.

It does not matter that Jesus was a Jew and not a Christian.

And forget about Jesus only mentioning two of the commandments, "Thou shall have no other Gods before me" and "thou shall not bear false witness against thy neighbor."

Those commandments do not seem to matter much. In fact, he repeats them again, especially the neighbor one. I wonder why? And the part about God being a forgiving God and a loving unconditional God does not seem to matter because again, people who take their own lives are not worthy of such love.

But I thought that all of us were not worthy.

Some folks believe that those who take their own life are not worthy of any reward and that at the eleventh hour, they blew it by taking their own life.

If they had not gotten right with God before the act they will be denied entry into Heaven. I wonder how the parents, sons, daughters, sisters, and brothers feel about their loved ones agonizing in eternal damnation.

The original title of this subchapter was going to be I'M NOT IN THE LIGHT, I AM THE LIGHT and that is how I want this subchapter to end.

By acknowledging that yes, it takes people who commit this act more time in the world of Spirit to find the light and gain knowledge, wisdom, and enlightenment to move on. They will see the errors of their ways at some point, learn the lessons that are put forth in front of them, and be able to move forward in order to achieve and obtain higher dimensions and ascension.

I am not here to say there is not a heaven or a hell. I do believe there is, but perhaps not in the way we think it is. Think of these 'places' as positions in our consciousness and depending upon the high ascension or the low descension determines how quickly or slowly someone will find the light.

You can say that those people are in a holding pattern or a lower dimension until they become lighter or maybe in a place some people might call purgatory. All I know is that they have to find more light and it will take some time but make no mistake about it, they will find the light eventually and then they will be able to say, "I'm not in the light . . . I am the light."

TAKE FIVE

This will be a tough one, but you can do it.

Take one deep, deep, deep breath, then very slowly exhale, letting it out until you almost feel exhausted and drained.

Assuming that you have been affected in some way by someone who has taken their own life, think of that person and just before you close your eyes give them permission to be forgiven and tell them that you love them, are thinking of them, and that you want them to move on in the Spirit realm.

Sit for a few minutes in silence and thank them for the time you knew them here on earth.

After you open your eyes, know that the Universe loves you, God is proud of you, and Spirit commends you for taking this step, as difficult and hard as it might have been, in giving that loved one so much needed light.

Peace.

NAVIGATING THE WAY FORWARD

There are three key quotes that will hopefully serve as a conclusion to the ideas presented in this book.

EMBRACE THE UNEXPLAINED—"Of course, that is not the whole story, but that is the way with stories; we make them what we will. It is a way of explaining the universe, while leaving the universe unexplained, it is a way of keeping it all alive, not boxing it into time."

—Jeanette Winterson

When we start to accept, even partially, those thoughts, ideas, places, and things that offer no rational explanation as to why they exist, is when we draw closer to obtaining sacredness on a higher level. This would be the start of our ascension path to enlightenment.

USE YOUR IMAGINATION—"We lay there and looked up at the night sky and she told me about stars called blue squares and red swirls and I told her I'd never heard of them. Of course not, she said, the important stuff they never tell you. You have to imagine it on your own."

—Brian Andreas

When I looked at this quote, what struck me was the innocence of the girl. It seemed to me that this girl, who appears to be connected to the Universe strongly, is pulling in wisdom from the other realm. Spirit is talking to her on a level, that is innocent, trustworthy, and sincere. Isn't that what imagination is all about? Imagination will never let us down if we are sincere in exploring it. Our imagination seeks a partnership with us. For this to happen, we have to be trustworthy and display a child-like innocence.

LOOK THROUGH THE WINDOW OF WISDOM—"To acquire knowledge, one must study; but to acquire wisdom, one must observe."

—Marilyn vos Savant

Study will only get us so far...observing everything around us and within us gives our soul and essence more windows to observe and inhale what the Universe is trying to teach us.

If we encounter any subject matter that is unexplainable, such as things that are beyond the veil...imagination and wisdom will be useful.

Imagine, observe, and embrace...these will be helpful when navigating the path that Spirit will lead you on.

Peace.

THE AUTHOR

Jerry McDaniel is a Clairvoyant, Psychic Medium, Intuitive, award-ing-winning author, blogger, and talk show radio host. His blogs have been viewed by thousands of people in over 80 countries.

He holds certifications in Natural Law, Mediumship, and Spiritualism and is a Certified Psychic Medium by two organizations, Oracle of the Age in South Carolina, and Open Arms Spiritual Church in Florida.

Jerry is a board member of THE SANCTUARY FOR MIND, BODY, AND SPIRIT located in Orlando and has worked with various organizations such as HELPING PARENTS HEAL and FROM GRIEF TO HOPE.

Jerry feels it is of the highest privilege to channel loved ones who have passed as well as read the vibrations of the Earth plane in order to see what messages the Universe has in store for the person(s) sitting in front of him.

Jerry is a practicing Catholic and lives in Orlando with his wife Mary.

CPSIA information can be obtained
at www.ICGtesting.com
Printed in the USA
FSHW021939210720

9 780998 826127